D1356627

C016577745

FINDING SISU

FINDING SISU

In Search of Courage, Strength
and Happiness the Finnish Way

Katja Pantzar

HODDER &
STOUGHTON

First published in Great Britain in 2018 by Hodder & Stoughton
An Hachette UK company
Published by arrangement with Katja Pantzar and Elina
Ahlback Literary Agency, Helsinki, Finland.

1

Copyright © Katja Pantzar 2018

The right of Katja Pantzar to be identified as the Author
of the Work has been asserted by her in accordance with
the Copyright, Designs and Patents Act 1988.

All rights reserved. No part of this publication may be reproduced, stored
in a retrieval system, or transmitted, in any form or by any means without
the prior written permission of the publisher, nor be otherwise circulated
in any form of binding or cover other than that in which it is published and
without a similar condition being imposed on the subsequent purchaser.

A CIP catalogue record for this title is available from the British Library

Hardback ISBN 978 1 473 66989 5
eBook ISBN 978 1 473 66992 5

Typeset in Avenir by Hewer Text UK Ltd, Edinburgh
Printed and bound in Great Britain by Clays Ltd, St Ives plc

Hodder & Stoughton policy is to use papers that are natural, renewable
and recyclable products and made from wood grown in sustainable
forests. The logging and manufacturing processes are expected to
conform to the environmental regulations of the country of origin.

Hodder & Stoughton Ltd
Carmelite House
50 Victoria Embankment
London EC4Y 0DZ

www.hodder.co.uk

For Felix

Contents

Introduction   1

1 Going Nordic: diving into an
  invigorating new lifestyle   13
2 In search of *sisu*: cultivating a *sisu* mindset   43
3 Cold-water cure: can winter swimming alleviate
  the symptoms of depression, stress and fatigue?   63
4 Soul of the sauna: sweat your way to better health   91
5 Nature therapy: the benefits of a walk in the woods   109
6 The Nordic diet: a simple and sensible
  approach to good health and weight loss   131
7 Getting a healthy start: cultivating *sisu*
  from early childhood   155
8 Pedalling to happiness – and health   183

9 The benefits of movement as medicine
  (and incidental exercise)   209
10 Nordic minimalism: creating a simpler
  and more sustainable lifestyle   239

  Conclusion: finding your *sisu*   263
  Epilogue   269
  Appendices   273
  Acknowledgements   279
  References   283

Introduction

~~~~

Large fluffy white snowflakes are falling from the night sky as three young men wearing terrycloth bathrobes run down a Helsinki street on a dark November evening. The crisp quiet air fills with the sound of their boisterous laughter and the crunch of snow under their slipper-clad feet.

For local residents, this is not an unusual sight. But for a relative newcomer like me, it's a striking scene to witness, especially against the urban backdrop of a capital city.

They sprint past the elegant centuries-old apartment blocks and head towards the water. On a small island just a stone's throw from downtown Helsinki, the presidential palace and the upscale design boutiques that line the Esplanade, these three young men are racing towards a nearby dock, from where they will swim.

Katja Pantzar

Over the time that I've lived here in the far north, I've heard about winter, or ice, swimming, the practice of taking dips in icy cold water in pursuit of its purported health benefits, which range from boosting immunity to reducing fatigue and stress.

As wild and crazy as the idea of voluntarily plunging into the Baltic Sea sounds, I decide at that moment that I must try it at least once – for those young men exude a joyful energy and hardiness that seems inextricably linked to their pastime.

To my great surprise when I eventually give it a try a few years later, winter swimming completely changes my life. By providing, over time, a natural remedy for the bouts of bone-crushing depression that I have suffered from since childhood, my icy dips, along with other elements of the Nordic lifestyle, help me to find my *sisu*, a unique Finnish form of resilience and perseverance in the face of adversity. This special courage arms me with tools to turn around my wellbeing and create a lifestyle that at last allows me to take charge of my life for the first time ever.

As I explore this concept of *sisu*, my journey of discovery is both personal and professional. As a writer and journalist I'm keenly interested in what makes people tick and curious about how they take care of their health

2

and wellbeing. Why do some people seem to thrive no matter what life throws at them, while others often seem to be hard done by? On a personal level, as someone who has struggled with depression and anxiety, I feel that this unique culture of resilience helps me transition from being a weaker, more passive, person scared of trying new things into someone who feels better and stronger both physically and mentally.

~~~

Fast forward to 2017 and I'm standing on the wooden dock that juts out into the Baltic Sea, the same spot that those young men were headed for so many dark nights ago.

As I climb down the metal ladder leading to a large hole of about three by three metres cut into the thick ice, I can see the city lights in the distance fringing the inky darkness. When I lower myself into the water, the cold shock – it's about 1 degree Celsius – hits me. During the first few strokes it feels like hundreds of pins and needles are pricking my body.

The pricks are soon replaced by a feeling of euphoria: 'I'm alive!' Following an invigorating swim of about thirty seconds, I pause for a moment at the bottom of the ladder, immersed up to my neck in the frigid water, before I climb back up onto the dock.

By now I have become a regular winter swimmer. I often take a quick dip on my way to or from work. Some might say I've developed an addiction. But I believe it's a healthy one. According to experts a thirty-second to one-minute dip has many of the same health benefits as going up and down stairs for fifteen to twenty minutes. My cold-water cure also boosts the hormones that are linked to feeling good such as endorphins, serotonin, dopamine and oxytocin. The practice is also known to improve the immune system's resistance, enhance circulation, burn calories and reduce stress.

As I walk up towards the shorefront building that houses the separate men's and women's saunas, showers and changing rooms, the rush of endorphins takes over and I no longer feel cold. My anxieties, stress, fatigue, and aches and pains have been left in the sea. In their place I feel a natural high as my body tingles all over, followed by a rush of warmth, and I get a surge of energy that makes me feel almost invincible.

Winter swimming has helped me tap into a deep reserve of strength and resilience I didn't know I possessed. Gone is the insecure, tired, want-to-pull-the-covers-over-my-head version of me. Where weakness once reigned, I've discovered my sense of *sisu*, the psychological power that allows me to pull myself together even when I feel mentally and physically depleted.

My fellow cold-water swimmers share the fantastic rush of endorphins and the triumphant feeling that comes post-dip: I'm greeted by exuberant, smiling people – contrary to the stereotypes of sombre Finns – boasting about how good they feel.

On this particular Thursday evening I have time to enjoy a post-swim treat: warming up in the quintessential Finnish steam bath, the sauna.

Peeling off my swimsuit, hat, gloves and slippers, I rinse off in the shower before stepping into the women's sauna where I ladle water from a bucket onto the stove's hot rocks. I sit in quiet meditation and bask in the warmth of the hot steam for a moment before joining in conversation with the other women who are sitting on the sauna's wooden benches.

If someone had told me ten, or even five, years ago that my ideal night out would involve jumping into icy seawater, I would have laughed out loud.

My former life in Toronto was far removed from nature's elements and did not include much self-care. My Thursday nights were comprised of little that could be described as wellness-related. A typical cocktail-fuelled night out with my media colleagues included stops at members-only bars and clubs. More often than not, that was preceded by some celebrity spotting at a launch or press event: I once shared a lift with actor Chris Noth, best known at the time as Mr Big on the hugely popular *Sex and the City* TV series; another evening I sat next to David Schwimmer (Ross on the hit sitcom *Friends*), while marvelling at how very petite the actress Minnie Driver, who was at the same party, was in real life.

While I'm a fan of both *SATC* and *Friends*, the notion that I once measured the success of a night by the number of drinks downed and VIPs spotted seems a lifetime ago now.

Yet an obsession with celebrity culture infused just about every aspect of life back then. Growing up in North America, it seemed perfectly normal – *de rigueur* in fact – that the majority of people I knew were on an endless quest for *the* magic self-improvement solution – usually in the form of an expensive and complicated new diet or exercise regime that would help them lose weight, get in shape, look and feel better, and work more efficiently. If the new regime was celebrity-endorsed, so that we might look like the stars, even better.

At the time, I shared the collective angst of many of my North American friends: I felt I was never skinny enough, beautiful enough or rich enough. It seemed to me that most of my problems would be solved if I could somehow magically achieve all three of those things.

I also shared another kind of anxiety, one that embarrassed me greatly for I erroneously perceived it to be a sign of weakness when I first received my diagnosis in my mid-twenties: depression.

Initially I made a doctor's appointment, convinced I had a grave life-threatening illness or some type of autoimmune disease. My symptoms had continued for weeks on end: I had no appetite, I was listless, I felt exhausted all the time but could not sleep, and none of the things that had previously brought me joy seemed to matter any more.

As I spoke with the sympathetic doctor, who ran a battery of medical tests and asked about what else was going on in my life, I began to cry. While I wept, I told her that the end of a serious romantic relationship had left me feeling very upset and as though I had failed somehow. That feeling of deep disappointment sparked a downward spiral and I started to view other aspects of my life from a similar perspective of ineptitude. Around the same time a family friend passed away after a long battle with cancer; their death deeply rattled me in a way that I could not fully explain at the time.

I later learned that a traumatic or stressful life event such as the end of a relationship, losing a job, or the death of a loved one can precipitate a depressive episode. If several triggers take place in a short space of time, it can increase the risk. It can happen to anyone.

I also know now that depression is incredibly common – the World Health Organisation (WHO) estimates that 300 million people worldwide suffer from it – but I didn't understand this at the time. While I finally had a name for those terrible gloomy spells that left me incapacitated and feeling so terribly low, as though I had been unplugged from the world and every cell in my body ached, instead of relief I felt a great sense of shame. Though I had suffered from dark spells since childhood, they had never been as crippling as this horrendous episode.

After all, what right did I have to be sad? At the time of my diagnosis, I was living in Vancouver, the much-touted

Canadian city on the West Coast, where I'd grown up in a middle-class family. I was living in my first rental apartment, I had paid off my student loan, I had a job as an editor and my social life was full of friends.

I lacked little. Yet I often felt utterly empty inside. Growing up in the '80s and '90s in a culture of convenience and consumerism, I looked for fulfilment in the wrong places and often equated it with external factors such as good looks and material possessions like expensive clothing and accessories or luxurious homes.

Some of my anxieties were also fuelled by my poor lifestyle – I didn't always eat regularly, exercise, follow a balanced diet (ice cream for dinner!) or rest enough.

The doctors I saw in Vancouver and later in Toronto prescribed antidepressants, anti-anxiety medication and psychotherapy. All of which helped pull me out of a very bad place, which I am grateful for to this day, but no medical practitioner ever really asked me how much time I spent outdoors being active or exercising or what my diet was like. No link was ever made between my poor lifestyle choices and my deepening depression.

I had a great many opportunities in Canada. After attending grad school in London, I worked as a writer and editor in Vancouver for a few years before moving to Toronto to work in book publishing.

Although I possessed many of the outward symbols of stability – a roof over my head, a permanent job, a boyfriend with a fancy car (and a small aeroplane!) and friends – I often felt profoundly anxious on the inside. A few years after my initial depression diagnosis, I came off antidepressants for several years, but had a prescription for anti-anxiety medication to deal with my recurring sense of unease. I couldn't seem to find a sense of peace or purpose. I often felt I was going through the motions – get dressed, go to work, attend parties, smile and behave like everything is okay – but inside I was a ball of nervous stress, worrying about everything from my relationships, finances and work to the meaning of life.

As a youngish woman in my late twenties and early thirties, I felt frustrated by the gender discrimination I experienced in the publishing and media industry. In one of my jobs I had several outrageous, but not uncommon, encounters. In addition to being evaluated on my appearance, on one occasion a male executive actually asked me how far I would go to secure the work of a top-name author. It was said with a laugh, but it felt salacious and just plain wrong.

As the only child of Finnish-Canadian immigrant parents, I had kept in touch with my roots, visiting Finland over the years. As I considered other work options, the Nordic ideal of equality – at the time Finland had its first female president – intrigued me. I had a European Union passport. What if I were to spend a year working in Finland?

Searching online I came across a posting in Helsinki that summed up a seemingly perfect job: English-language magazine editor – must be willing and able to edit, write and possibly travel.

The opportunity to live in Europe appealed greatly. I could learn new skills and see the world.

When I was offered the position on a temporary contract, I jumped at the opportunity. At the time, I thought I would stay in Finland for a year or two, brush up on my Finnish (my family emigrated to Canada from Finland via New Zealand in the 1970s) and learn a bit more about my roots.

I certainly never thought that I would end up falling in love with the no-nonsense Nordic lifestyle, build a career and a life, get married and have a child there.

At that point I had yet to discover the Finns' unique quality of resilience – *sisu* – and all that it would later reveal to me.

Regardless of where we live or what we do, we all face struggles and challenges in our daily lives and we could all benefit from some extra courage and fortitude. In these pages, I will share with you what I have learned – the simple and sensible ways with which I've found my *sisu* and how you can introduce them into your life so you can find your *sisu* too.

For it was through this concept that I uncovered the many elements of the pared-down Nordic lifestyle that helped me to significantly improve my overall wellbeing.

CHAPTER 1

Going Nordic: diving into an invigorating new lifestyle

During my first few months in Finland, my everyday life undergoes a transformation, a makeover. It's not an extreme makeover; there is no dramatic new regime. But as my new day-to-day routine takes shape, a lifestyle slowly but surely emerges, almost without me really noticing.

Instead of working late into the evening as I often did in Toronto, my workday in Helsinki starts around 9 a.m. and ends around 5 p.m. There's a proper lunch-hour break, which just about everyone seems to take at a café nearby or in the staff canteen that serves up a hot meal that the company helps subsidise. There are always several dishes to choose from: vegetarian, chicken, fish or meat, in addition to a plentiful salad bar and an assortment of freshly baked breads.

Though anyone who has eaten at workplace canteens in Finland would likely laugh at the notion of them resembling the Nordic diet – it is undeniably mass-catered food made for hundreds of employees – the dishes on offer do loosely follow the tenets of it. Which is: simple, affordable food that emphasises local and seasonable products – vegetables, fruits, berries, wholegrains such as oats and rye, fish, game and dairy. The dessert on offer is often a piece of fruit or quark with blueberries – it is rarely cake or pastries.

This new routine of taking a proper lunch break also creates the opportunity for changing my eating habits: rather than having my main meal in the evening, I now have it in the middle of the day – as millions of Scandinavians do. Instead of scarfing down a sandwich over my keyboard, as I had previously done, I sit with my colleagues and eat a proper, fairly balanced meal while we discuss the issues of the day. Rather than spending the day hungry in anticipation of a late dinner, I'm well fuelled.

I start riding a bicycle to work, as many of my co-workers do. Initially I cycle on a forty-year-old bright blue Jopo, a sturdy Finnish-design classic with no gears, lent to me by my aunt and uncle. This no-frills bike symbolises Nordic simplicity and design – a bike doesn't need to have a million gears to move forward.

In several cities where I've lived, I've ridden (or tried to ride) my bicycle to school or work. But in London, Toronto and Vancouver, I found it much more difficult to do so because there wasn't always a network of well-marked and maintained bike paths leading to the places I needed to go, and jostling with busy traffic made me nervous. This is changing though: cities around the world have made massive strides over the last decade in promoting cycling as a form of transport.

In Helsinki, as in the other Nordic capitals, there's a series of marked bike paths throughout the city; often a painted line divides the pavement – one side for pedestrians, the other for cyclists.

I quickly become seriously hooked on cycling. It's such a practical way to get around and it provides me with daily exercise without the extra effort required to go to the gym after a long workday. My six-kilometre route through woods, city and along the seaside in the fresh air wakes me up in the morning. I start to observe nature and the changing seasons in a way I've not done before. I notice that I sleep better at night, which in turn seems to reduce my levels of anxiety.

After work, I pedal away the day's stress. I soon realise that when I don't bike to work, I miss it and feel lethargic.

Instead of taking a coffee break, some of my colleagues go swimming or aqua-jogging – running in the water with a buoyancy belt; they head down to the staff pool for fifteen minutes of exercise and return refreshed, physically and mentally. I decide to try it out and occasionally join them, discovering the benefits of increased energy and concentration.

These are just a few of the lifestyle changes that I find myself making, naturally and almost without noticing.

Finland is, of course, also full of private gyms offering everything from personal trainers to spinning classes, CrossFit and yoga. But my first impression is that for a great many people, exercise and wellbeing are largely equated with simple and sensible options such as walking, biking and swimming that are accessible to everyone, and that can become a natural, almost incidental part of the day's routine, rather than a forced add-on.

Hello *sisu*!

Underlining just about every aspect of my gradual immersion into the Nordic lifestyle – which I must confess takes me a while to adjust to and fully appreciate ('Wait, we're having a team-building day outdoors in a nature park? But it's snowing!') – is the unique Finnish strength of will, a determination not to give up or take the easy way out. That is, having oodles of *sisu*.

Initially, I mistake this *sisu* quality for stubbornness, eccentricity or a thriftiness that seems foreign and totally unnecessary to me.

For example, having grown up in a cars-rule culture, I'm elated that one of the perks of being employed by a large media company means a taxi allowance to travel to work functions such as interviews, press events and the airport for assignments abroad.

Yet to my great bewilderment, a colleague of mine – who has the same taxi benefit – frequently opts to cycle to work events that are within a reasonable distance instead of hopping into a company-paid cab.

At the time I'm truly perplexed. Why on earth would someone voluntarily choose to take the less easy way out? Pedalling instead of relaxing in the comfort of a chauffeured ride?

Much later I understand their decision comes from Nordic practicality topped with a healthy dose of grit. After being in the office for several hours, what better than a little bit of exercise and fresh air? Not to mention the environmental benefits of one less car on the road. And sometimes the pedalling option may actually be faster if it means zipping along unhindered in the bicycle lane rather than sitting in rush-hour traffic.

With hindsight I consider many of those examples set by my colleagues and other people I've met in Finland to be small daily acts of *sisu*.

But it's a long journey before I arrive at this conclusion.

The unique Finnish strength of will, a determination not to give up or take the easy way out

One of the first times that I pay attention to the term *sisu* is when I start winter cycling during the second winter of my stay. As I brave freezing temperatures and snow, a neighbour who sees me pulling up on my bicycle in the courtyard of our apartment building says to me: '*Olet sisukas!*'– 'You have courage!' I take this as a compliment and translate it to mean that I'm a badass who has *sisu* because I'm doing something physically demanding in challenging weather conditions. Later, my winter swimming practice also generates this same phrase of praise.

I had previously heard the word *sisu*, but never really given it much thought. I begin to realise that *olet sisukas* means more than just being a badass and later I decide to find out more about the term that appears just about everywhere in Finland. It's the brand name of a much-loved liquorice pastille that's been around since 1928. *Sisu* is also part of the country's unofficial motto or slogan: '*Sisu,* sauna and Sibelius', which I think is intended to sum up the essence of the country and its identity.

Now, sauna and Sibelius seem self-explanatory.

The country is brimming with saunas, private and public – estimates place the total at some 3.3 million saunas in a country of 5.5 million people – and the Finnish steam bath's role as a quintessential part of the lifestyle and culture is indisputable. In fact, it's almost impossible to visit Finland and avoid the sauna experience, or at least an invitation to one.

As for Sibelius, that's Jean Sibelius (1865–1957), one of Finland's best-known composers. His many accomplishments include composing the defiant 'Finlandia' – an unofficial national anthem that was forbidden during Russian rule, which ended in 1917. Finland's independence is a massive point of pride for the Finns, who were ruled for six centuries by the Swedes before the country became part of the Russian Empire as a Grand Duchy in 1809. This also perhaps explains the Finns' competitiveness with the Swedes in everything from ice hockey to international rankings of any kind.

But when it comes to the essence of *sisu*, its definition appears to be more elusive. When I ask people what they think it means, I get a range of answers that could best be summed up with an unofficial consensus of:

'It's about not giving up, especially when things get tough.'

Finns often go on to cite significant *sisu* achievements such as great victories in war and sport.

The most commonly referred to is Finland's triumph over the Soviet Union during the Winter War. In 1940, *Time* magazine eloquently described that unique quality of resilience:

'The Finns have something they call *sisu*. It is a compound of bravado and bravery, of ferocity and tenacity, of the ability to keep fighting after most people would have quit, and to fight with the will to win. The Finns translate *sisu* as "the Finnish spirit", but it is a much more gutful word than that.'

The Winter War conflict began in November 1939 with the Soviet invasion of Finland and ended with the Moscow Peace Treaty in March 1940. Although the Soviets had 3 times more soldiers, 30 times more aircraft, and 100 times more tanks, the Finnish army managed to outsmart and deter the Soviet army in brutal winter temperatures as low as minus 40 degrees Celsius at a time of year when the far north was blanketed by darkness for most of the day.

The images of Finnish soldiers on skis in their white uniforms, a simple but clever camouflage against the snowy backdrop, became a symbol of the special kind of resilience and strength in persevering in the face of the seemingly impossible. Despite being outnumbered by the Soviets on just about every front, the Finns persisted and won peace. Though Finland had to cede some territory to the Soviets, the tiny Nordic nation maintained its independence against a much larger power.

Other popular *sisu* examples include amazing sporting feats, such as that of Finnish Olympic runner Lasse Virén's unbelievable comeback after falling during the 10,000-metre race at the 1972 Munich Summer Olympics. Not only did Virén get up and continue to run, he went on to win the gold medal – and set a new world record. Now that is true *sisu*, as many Finns tell me.

But is *sisu* culturally specific? Or can anyone build up their resilience Finnish-style?

Framing *sisu* within the context of my own quest for a healthier and ultimately happier life greatly interests me.

I believe that tapping into a reserve of grit or resilience that I didn't know I had – whether by making the effort to go for a cold-water swim each morning or by getting on my bike whatever the weather – has been fundamental in providing me with the tools to boost my mental and physical wellbeing. It has enabled me to move away from 'learned helplessness' – an attitude where I thought there was little I could do but accept myself as a slightly lethargic depressive who sometimes had difficulty getting out of bed in the morning – into someone who wakes up early to squeeze in a dip before the day starts.

In my search to better understand the concept of *sisu*, I have come up with a list of questions. Is *sisu* a mental power or muscle that you flex? Where does it come from? Is it a cultural construct, part of a country brand or a slogan? Or, as I suspect, a sort of mind-and-body attitude that anyone, anywhere, can tap into? In my quest to wrap my head around the term, I initially apply it liberally to cover a quality that I notice a great many Finns seem to share: a hardy, active, outdoors-in-any-weather, do-it-yourself (DIY) approach to life.

Even when it comes to domestic chores such as house or window cleaning, which many people could easily afford to pay someone else to do, it seems instead to be a source of personal pride and satisfaction to take on the task oneself.

Is *sisu* a mental power or muscle that you flex?

I observe that this DIY approach also includes trying to fix things before rushing out to buy new ones, and taking on home renovations instead of contracting them out. Doing instead of buying.

As for this special hardiness, I notice that it appears to link into a kind of experiences-over-possessions attitude. For example, during a typical Monday lunch, many of my co-workers talk about activities they undertook over the weekend. Shopping or discussing material acquisitions rarely form the answer to the question 'How was your weekend?' or 'What did you do?' Instead, the most common responses include outdoor- or nature-based activities, regardless of the weather or season: 'We were in the woods picking berries and/or mushrooms; fishing at the cottage; swimming at the lake; skiing; or on a mini-break in Stockholm, Tallinn, London or Berlin.'

It's not that I wasn't exposed to outdoorsy types growing up in Canada, but here in Finland a daily dose of nature seems to form part of nearly everyone's lexicon. This is in part a reflection of Finland's relatively late urbanisation during the 1950s and 1960s. Prior to the Second World War, 75 per cent of Finns lived in rural areas; now almost 85 per cent of the population lives in cities and urban areas. But more than that, it seems that a great love and appreciation of the outdoors is in the DNA.

Nordic simplicity

As time goes on, when I return to North America on visits I'm struck by how complicated urban life seems to be on so many levels.

On a rainy December day in Vancouver, I watch as my friend's active six-year-old son practically climbs the walls of their townhouse. When my friend says that perhaps he needs medication to help him calm down, I look at her in disbelief and as tactfully as I can suggest that he probably just needs to go outside and run and jump and play. 'It's normal for a young child to be full of energy,' I say, trying to reassure her. Her response? She doesn't want to take him outside because they would get wet.

From a Nordic perspective, it seems odd to me that her first thought was medication, not exercise or activity, and that she didn't think to invest in good raingear. Especially since Vancouver is one of Canada's rainiest cities, with upwards of 150 days of rain a year on average.

Another time in the same city, I'm waiting for a dear friend in a café. When he arrives out of breath, complaining about traffic and how hard it was to find a parking spot, my first thought is to ask him why he didn't walk or hop on a bus as he lives only a few kilometres away.

I don't ask the question, partly because I fear it will sound condescending, but partly because I think I already know the answer. We both grew up at a time in North America in the late '80s and '90s when owning a car was (and in many places still is) an extension of your personality, a fundamental right. The idea of not driving a car just wasn't, and still isn't, entertained.

From my new viewpoint it also seems that many people have an overly complicated and costly relationship with other areas of wellbeing such as diet and exercise.

A friend in New York is always experimenting with new diets, from low-carb to high-carb to no-carb or whatever the trend of the moment is. One of the most bizarre is a powdered soup-only diet delivered weekly to her door by courier in special, just-add-water packs. Another friend has tried everything from a just-peanut-butter diet to a chicken-only one. Add to that colonic irrigation, celebrity-endorsed fasts and all manner of detox cleanses.

Every time someone enthuses about their latest diet – which this time is 'going to change everything' – I find myself thinking the same thing: 'It sounds unhealthy and impossible to stick to. Why not just eat a sensible balanced diet and cut out the biscuits, cakes and sugary drinks?'

In stark contrast, many of the Scandinavians I meet seem to share a simple, few-frills common-sense approach to health and wellbeing. Of course there are people who undertake extreme diets and exercise programmes, but often when a Finnish colleague or friend has lost weight and is asked how they did it, the answer runs along the lines of: 'I cut out extra desserts and late-night snacking, ate more vegetables and became more active by taking up swimming or going for more walks.' Rarely do people say they have been on the diet or exercise fad of the moment.

This is not to suggest that there is anything bad in finding an exercise or diet programme that works for you and is enjoyable. But it seems that a great many people have outsourced their wellbeing to expensive, time-consuming, hard-to-stick-to programmes that don't work and actually may not be that healthy.

There are fewer very overweight people in Finland and next door in Sweden and in Norway, compared with some other parts of the developed world. As of 2014, more than 1.9 billion adults worldwide are now classified as overweight, according to the WHO, which has called it an epidemic.

This doesn't mean that slim equals healthy, but there are real health risks associated with carrying around excess weight, including high blood pressure, which can lead to coronary heart disease, type 2 diabetes and other lifestyle illnesses.

In Finland, I come to notice all kinds of positive attitudes that relate to wellbeing and body image.

The Scandinavians seem to have far fewer hang-ups about their bodies. Nordic men or women may not be entirely happy with their figure, but they don't seem to be waging a war with their bodies like many North Americans and Brits I've met.

Perhaps Finns feel more at ease with their body image because they've grown up in a sauna culture. The sauna, essentially a steam bath also known as the 'poor man's pharmacy', is the ultimate in relaxation and cleansing – you sweat out toxins while sitting in the warm steam.

In ancient times, the sauna was a revered place. Women gave birth there, since the heat made it one of the most sterile places to deliver a baby in those days. Studies have shown that the Finnish sauna, in addition to soothing and relaxing muscles by releasing endorphins, can relieve pain and help to prevent dementia.

What strikes me is that the sauna is also a great leveller. If you grow up seeing people naked, nudity is not such a big deal. You also grow up with the knowledge that bodies come in all sizes and shapes. *That's* normal and natural, not the stylised images of 'perfect' bodies as seen on social media or in glossy magazines.

There is another significant aspect of the Finnish sauna: equality. There's no VIP system; former presidents sit beside shop clerks. In a way, the sauna represents the non-hierarchical nature of Nordic society. A popular Finnish quote sums this up: 'All men are created equal; but nowhere more so than in a sauna.'

It seems that almost everyone I meet in the Nordics is culturally programmed to spend time in nature all year round; in summer and winter, particularly, they rest, restore and recharge at the family cottage.

The majority of Finns seem to know which mushrooms and berries are edible and how to pick them, a very handy skill to have, especially during economic downturns. If you live in an apartment and don't have your own garden, there are thousands of allotments or community gardens (*siirtolapuutarhat*), throughout the country. Anyone can rent or purchase a small plot of land and grow a plate of local greens.

Long before it became an international trend, the concept of local food has been embedded in the Nordic way of life.

Nordic wellbeing

As 'wellbeing' and 'lifestyle' have become buzzwords, the international press has devoted more column inches to examining the differences in quality of life in countries around the world.

In 2017, the World Happiness Report, from the UN's Sustainable Development Solutions Network, ranked

Finland as one of the world's top five happiest countries along with Nordic neighbours Denmark, Iceland, and Norway.

And in 2016, Finland was named the most progressive country in the world. According to the Social Progress Index by the American non-profit Social Progress Imperative, all the Nordic countries are in the top ten, with Finland at number one.

What's fascinating about the Social Progress Index is that it doesn't include GDP, but instead ranks social and environmental indicators based on 'basic human needs, foundations of wellbeing, and opportunity'.

What grabs my attention is the think-tank's definition of social progress: 'The capacity of a society to meet the basic human needs of its citizens, establish the building blocks that allow citizens and communities to enhance and sustain the quality of their lives, and create the conditions for all individuals to reach their full potential.'

That definition resonates with me. The Finnish infrastructure and social safety net has helped me to create a healthy and functional lifestyle that has allowed my husband and I to raise a son while working full-time. I've also been fortunate career-wise. For many years I worked with a large media company before I made the decision to go freelance. My work as a writer, editor and broadcast journalist has allowed me to see the world. I've also had career opportunities, including a stint as a TV news presenter that started when I was in my forties, which I'm not sure would have presented itself in countries where opinions about age and on-air looks reign.

Many positive elements of the Nordic lifestyle that I have discovered provide an excellent primer for an easier, healthier, more sustainable and balanced life that is in touch with the natural world.

I also notice Finland ranking high in other international comparisons. In 2017 Finland was named the most stable country in the world, according to the Fragile States Index; the freest country in the world together with Sweden and Norway; and the safest country in the world according to the World Economic Forum's Travel and Tourism Competitiveness Report 2017.

Finland is by no means perfect – no place is. There are many challenging aspects to life here, including the long, cold and dark winters that are accompanied by a special kind of melancholy that places in the North seem to share, the sombre mood often captured in Nordic noir literature and TV.

While Finland is a tech leader – known as the birthplace of Nokia, Linux and Supercell, along with numerous digital health solutions – it is in the natural, offline Nordic lifestyle choices that I have found the greatest sense of wellbeing and *sisu*. These are inexpensive, simple solutions that don't require special apps, gadgets or expensive equipment and are largely accessible to a great many people regardless of time or budgetary constraints.

Around the world we are all grappling with so many of the same issues, from environmental concerns and uncertainty about the future, to the health risks associated with sedentary lifestyles.

Many positive elements of the Nordic lifestyle that I have discovered provide an excellent primer for an easier, healthier, more sustainable and balanced life that is in touch with the natural world.

And just about all of these elements can be tapped into anywhere in the world, as I will go on to show throughout this book. Each chapter that follows is devoted to a specific topic and how it can serve to strengthen your *sisu*.

In the land of the midnight sun

Contrary to popular belief, it's not always cold in Finland. In addition to the almost endless light during the summer months owing to the country's geographical location near the top of the world, the weather can – occasionally – be warm. Like it was during the five-week-long heatwave a few summers ago, when the mercury tipped over 25 degrees Celsius for more than thirty-five days straight.

On a weekday evening in early August during that hot summer, I'm on the shores of the Helsinki island, Katajanokka, where I live with my family. I'm a few minutes' walk further east from my winter swimming dock, past the rows of pastel-coloured Art Nouveau apartment blocks and opposite the off-duty ice-breakers – ships designed to break through ice and create a navigable passage – with their quirky Finnish names such as our very own *Sisu*, *Urho* (brave), and *Voima* (power) that ply the Baltic during the winter months.

There's a small group of us, mostly folks from the neighbourhood, on and around the wooden dock, a spot traditionally used for washing rag rugs (made of discarded clothing and household fabrics) with natural pine soap. This Finnish custom dates back generations and though there have been plans to phase it out due to concerns over the soap's effects on the seawater, the docks remain.

As half a dozen kids happily cheer each other on as they jump from the dock's wooden railings into the sea, I'm cooling off in the water with my good friend Tiina.

We both laugh when a little blond-haired boy assumes a series of superhero poses on the railings, before launching his strong but tiny body into the sea.

The nature link

A journalist, Tiina is in her fifties, though she looks more than a decade younger. She exudes a healthful beauty and possesses an inspiring energy like many of the women I meet in Finland. Like them, she is well educated, well travelled and speaks several languages.

In addition to overlapping career interests, we share a great many things in common, including our mutual admiration of each other's children (Tiina has two kids, I have a young son), sea swimming year round (through her I was first introduced to winter swimming) and cycling just about everywhere. I decide to use her as a sounding board for some of my questions about Nordic wellbeing because she is constructively critical by profession and humble by nature in that 'we're nothing special' manner that typifies her generation of Finns.

From my North American perspective, it's a luxury to live so centrally in a capital city and to be able to cycle or walk just about everywhere. Our island has a mix of rental and owned apartments and you don't need to be wealthy to live here.

If I lived in the city where I grew up I would likely spend two or three hours a day driving to and from work. This would add up to at *least* ten hours a week, or forty hours a month, spent in a car. Instead, depending on the day, I spend about thirty minutes to an hour or more outdoors on my bike getting some fresh air and exercise while 'commuting'.

Given my own gradual realisation of the link between daily doses of nature and my wellness, I ask Tiina if she thinks this connection with nature keeps people in Finland healthy and aware of the bigger environmental picture. She pauses for a second, thinking, and then nods.

'In general, yes. For me, getting outdoors is essential to my mental and physical wellbeing,' she replies. 'When I was in my early thirties I realised that if I didn't get outdoors every day, I literally felt as though I would wither away. So long as I kept physically active by skiing in the winter, swimming, taking exercise classes and cycling everywhere, I felt so much better, healthier and stronger,' she says.

Part of what enables cycling and swimming in the sea all year round is the Nordic infrastructure, which is based on the principle once referred to as 'the welfare state of a shared common good'. That means less income disparity and slightly higher taxes, with the idea that everyone should have access to childcare, healthcare, education and other benefits such as acesss to large areas of green.

It does cross my mind that I may be living in some sort of a Helsinki hippy bubble.

So I pose the question to Tiina. Are we incredibly lucky to live in this natural urban environment, or is this how life is for most people who live in the capital?

'It's funny you should put it that way,' she says. 'Of course we're fortunate, but the connection with nature is such a normal part of life for Finns – it's in our genes – that we take it for granted.

'Nature is everywhere, and access to it is embedded in the public infrastructure.'

Helsinki is one of the few European capitals surrounded almost entirely by sea, with 100 kilometres of shoreline and about 330 islands dotting the waterfront. There are numerous summer swimming beaches and winter swimming spots around the compact city centre and in the suburbs and countryside.

By comparison, the waterfronts of many capital cities around the world are polluted or the shoreline has been built up, restricting access to the water.

Tiina points out that in Helsinki, as in many Nordic cities, it's easy to get by without a car. 'The infrastructure supports not having a car through an efficient rapid transit network. City planners are constantly working to make the city more accessible for people walking and biking,' she says.

In addition to maintaining bicycle paths all year round – including clearing the cycling lanes of snow during the winter months – the City of Helsinki has linked its bike-share scheme into the public transit system. That means travel cards can be used to borrow a bicycle.

In the capital region and throughout the country, there are huge swathes of public parks and forests. A concept called 'Everyman's Right' (*jokamiehen oikeus*) means that everyone can walk, ski or cycle in the countryside so long as they don't harm the natural environment or landowner's property. Everyone is also permitted to swim in both inland waters and the sea. (Picking berries, herbs and mushrooms is also allowed.)

Tiina and I finish our swim in the late evening sunlight – the sun is a large orange orb just above the horizon.

At this time of year there are about seventeen hours of sunlight a day in Helsinki. The sun, which rose at 5 a.m. this morning, will set just after 10 p.m.

We climb up onto the dock where we dry ourselves off and briefly chat with a few people we know. Then we walk up to the lawn near the birch trees where our bikes are parked and say our goodbyes before cycling off to our respective homes.

As I pedal home, the idea of building extra strength – mental and physical – through activity, specifically outdoor recreation, stays with me. My experience has been similar to Tiina's – the more I get outdoors the better I feel.

Before I moved to Finland, my disconnect with forests and nature no doubt partly fuelled my depression and anxiety; it just wasn't part of the fabric of my everyday life. Researchers the world over from Stanford University to the University of Helsinki have found evidence that city folk who spend little time in nature or natural environments suffer a higher incidence of depression and anxiety and other mental illnesses.

Back in 2005, American author Richard Louv's ground-breaking bestseller *Last Child in the Woods* coined the term 'nature-deficit disorder', referring to the myriad of health problems, many psychological, that children suffer because they spend so much time indoors, often in a virtual world, and not enough time outdoors.

In addition to the nature link, Tiina's comment about feeling stronger goes beyond the notion of merely physical strength and ties into the unique Finnish sense of fortitude.

City folk who spend little time in nature or natural environments suffer a higher incidence of depression and anxiety and other mental illnesses.

I later message Tiina to ask her what she thinks *sisu* means.

'My first thought is that I'm not totally sure what it means; but then a kind of macho, masculine quality comes to mind. On further thought, I would actually say that women are damn full of *sisu*; they are persistent, stubborn, and shoulder all kinds of responsibilities. In the Finnish context, there have been historic reasons for that: men went into the woods, away for work or war, and women were left to take care of a great many things, from running a farm to a family business, and the household and children,' she replies.

When I ask her if she thinks *sisu* is connected to wellbeing, she says it brings to mind the older cross-country skiers in their seventies and eighties whom she sees throughout the country, who are in excellent shape and have great endurance.

As we further discuss the idea, Tiina expands on it: 'Though *sisu* can be linked to sports, for me it's a kind of daily stamina and resilience to keep everything running, even through life's grey patches. It's not about being competitive, like winning a marathon. It's about surviving and thriving in daily life.'

So is it a Finnish quality, I ask?

'No, not necessarily,' she replies. 'But it is Nordic. If I think of the North American crime-novel tradition, when the heroine gets beaten, she goes home and pours a bath and a glass of whiskey. In the Nordic version, the same heroine would go for a winter swim and head to the sauna to lick her wounds; there would be less striving for heroism and more effort and focus on just getting ahead.'

Although Tiina and I are both adults with demanding careers, bills to pay and families to care for, it occurs to me that on many levels we live somewhat fairy-tale lives.

The thought comes to mind as I read a bedtime story to my then four-year-old son. Perhaps it's because my young son is cuddled up beside me, but somehow our youthful lives on a little island by the sea brings to mind the popular Swedish–Finnish fairy tales featuring those loveable Moomins, who embark on adventures in the natural world with a sense of curiosity and wonder.

Originally a popular children's book series, the Moomin stories by writer and artist Tove Jansson (1914–2001) became a comic strip commissioned by the Associated Press in 1948, and was adapted into cartoons, movies, and TV series. The analogy seems fitting, as Jansson lived on our Katajanokka island as a child. In fact, her life and work have recently been commemorated by naming a park after her that's just down the street from where we live.

And those original Moomin stories carry doses of *sisu*, too. Little My, the fiercely independent, brave and mischievous little girl who is adopted by the Moomins, always manages to get herself out of a tight spot – no matter what happens.

DIY daily *sisu*

- Cycle or walk to work or school, or part of the way, if possible.
- First try to fix or mend items instead of throwing them away and buying new ones.
- Adopt simple daily habits such as taking the stairs instead of the elevator.
- Winter and challenging weather conditions happen in many parts of the world: bundle up and embrace the elements.
- If you usually outsource some of your domestic chores, try doing them yourself for a week.
- Introduce some nature into your weekend – a walk in the woods, a trip to the beach, planting some herbs in the garden, or even outdoor swimming.

CHAPTER 2

In search of *sisu*: cultivating a *sisu* mindset

Long before I discover how much we are affected by our environment and our daily habits, one of my first salves for when I feel down is reading. Thankfully, my wise parents instilled in me a love of literature and, from early on – age five or six – I became a voracious reader.

Stories and books both inspire and sustain me, often providing a much-needed escape when that familiar sense of ennui starts to circle.

One of my first childhood memories is sitting cross-legged in my blue denim pinafore and orange T-shirt in the morning circle of first grade at elementary school. We start singing the ABC song and I sigh internally as I think to myself: is this really *it*? Are we going to be singing the ABC song for the rest of our lives?

But then salvation arrives as the teacher begins to read us Maurice Sendak's magical *Where the Wild Things Are*. As she turns the illustrated pages, I'm overcome by excitement, relief, and the feeling that things may actually turn out to be okay after all. For through the adventure-filled children's classic about a solitary boy called Max who is liberated by his imagination, I feel a wonderful sense of hope.

Finding a lifeline through literature is a theme that continues into my adolescence and adulthood.

The second seminal moment in my reading therapy is the discovery of a thick stack of *New Yorker* magazines at a friend's family cottage on the Gulf Islands off the mainland of British Columbia. It's the late '80s and I am an awkward and insecure teenager curious about the world. As I pore over those pages of the *New Yorker*, a whole new cosmopolitan world opens up to me and those back issues serve as an introduction to writing, storytelling, and journalism – and the idea of a possible career.

Almost a quarter of a century later on the other side of the globe it's the *New Yorker* that provides me with my first concrete link between the idea of *sisu* and joy.

In the spring of 2016, the *New Yorker* published an article entitled 'The Glossary of Happiness'. In it, writer Emily Anthes recounts how Tim Lomas, a lecturer in applied positive psychology at the University of East London, was inspired by the word *sisu* to create his Positive Lexicography Project. According to the article, it set off the idea there must be words in other languages, which have no direct translation in English, that describe positive traits.

According to the piece, Lomas heard a presentation on *sisu* given by Emilia Lahti, a doctoral student at Aalto University in Helsinki at an International Positive Psychology Conference.

In her article, Anthes defines *sisu* as being similar to, but not the same as, perserverance or grit. And Lomas observed that Lahti saw *sisu* as a universal quality.

Thanks to the *New Yorker*, I find what I've been looking for: possibly one of the world's foremost *sisu* researchers, Emilia Lahti.

Katja Pantzar

When I first meet Lahti, she's one of the keynote speakers at a *sisu* seminar held in Helsinki by the Finnish Academy of Science and Letters as part of Finland's 100th anniversary of independence celebrations.

As she takes to the stage, Lahti, in her mid-thirties, smiles warmly and radiates an infectious positivity that lights up the room. Dressed in a black blouse, jeans and boots, with a sports watch on her wrist – she's also an ultra marathon runner – Lahti introduces herself as a researcher and social activist with an interest in applied positive psychology and social justice, who holds a master's degree in social psychology and a master of applied positive psychology degree. She studied with positive psychology pioneer Dr Martin Seligman, the author of bestsellers including *Authentic Happiness* and *Flourish* and who is credited with, among numerous other achievements, the theory of 'learned helplessness'.

It was while studying at the University of Pennsylvania that Lahti came up with her pioneering *sisu* research under the mentorship of academic and psychologist Dr Angela Duckworth, author of the bestseller *Grit: The Power of Passion and Perseverance*.

Lahti, in her presentation, characterises the ancient Finnish construct as relating to mental toughness and the

46

ability to endure significant stress, while taking action against seemingly impossible odds: 'In its native country, *sisu* is a way of life, a philosophy, which has impacted the lives of generations of people.' She explains that the word literally means 'guts'. '*Sisus* in Finnish is something inside.' She goes on to quote the composer Sibelius: '*Sisu* is like a metaphorical shot in the arm that allows the individual to do what's impossible.'

As Lahti relates her own story, she credits Duckworth, her mentor, who guided her as a young grad student. 'Angela saw something in me and my work. As I pondered my research topics, she encouraged me to follow the one that would focus on *sisu*.'

As I sit in the grand conference room in the House of Estates, one of central Helsinki's most regal buildings, I recognise a familiar theme in Lahti's account. It's one that I've come across numerous times. Finns, in their humbleness, are often unaware of how interesting, exemplary, or unique some of their concepts are. It often takes an outsider – in this case Duckworth – to point out how fascinating or worthy of research a Finnish concept might be.

As Lahti highlights her research and findings, one of her definitions of *sisu* – 'the importance of being in situations

that test us and allow us to see what we're capable of'–
echoes so many other people's descriptions to me of what
they think this Finnish fortitude means.

~~~~~~

Like many people who are passionate about what they do,
Lahti also has a personal interest in her research. In her
case, she is a survivor of domestic violence, which led to
her interest in this ability to overcome great adversity.

As an ultra-marathon runner, Lahti follows a gruelling
training schedule. As I listen to her presentation I wonder:
does a strong body build a strong mind that in turn
enables more *sisu*? From my own experience, I certainly
think so.

Later, as I ponder this question, I call André Noël Chaker,
a Canadian-born lawyer and one of Finland's top public
speakers, an entrepreneur and author, who has carved out
a very successful career for himself here in Finland over the
past two decades. As he has devoted an entire chapter to
the topic of *sisu* in one his Finnish bestsellers, *The Finnish
Miracle: 100 Years of Success*, I ask him whether being
physically strong helps build up that special resilience.
'Definitely,' he replies. 'My whole life here has been

learning about *sisu*, about not giving up – to that end I have been an avid winter swimmer, marathon runner and triathlete.'

In a 2014 TEDx talk, Chaker provides an apt definition of *sisu*: 'Icy cold determination that makes you do the impossible.'

~~~~~~

About a month later, Emilia Lahti and I connect via Skype to talk further.

I ask her about the mind–body connection to *sisu*. Does physical wellbeing in the form of good health and a strong body affect psychological *sisu* strength?

'That's really a core question to me nowadays,' she replies. 'When I started researching the concept of *sisu*, I looked at it through the lens of psychology and the mind. It's really only recently that we are slowly starting to see more research on "embodied cognition".' Embodied cognition theory holds that the body influences the mind.

Lahti says that she only realised the connection between the body and the mind at the start of 2017.

Part of the issue, she explains, is that previously she was defining *sisu* as a non-cognitive quality like grit.

Non-cognitive refers to attitudes and behaviours such as integrity and compassion, which don't require our thinking and are not directly related to our intelligence.

Struggling to write a research paper one night, she decided to stop and turn in. 'In my gut I knew that I was missing something really important,' she says.

Then Lahti recounts how during the early hours of the morning everything changed.

'All of a sudden my entire brain lit up: the answer had been right in front of me all this time. I thought back to the interviews and data I'd collected from the 2013 study I did. It had 1,208 Finnish and Finnish-American respondents, a high figure for a mainly qualitative survey – and I realised the connection that was so obvious,' she explains.

'When people talk about *sisu* and they're trying to describe it, they point to their gut, like it's literally in there – they don't point to their hearts or heads.

'The clue is in the word *sisus*, which [in Finnish] is literally the interior, or inside of a thing or a being. Then it hit me that *sisu* is like the somatic embodiment of mental toughness. What we attribute to the mind – our strength and ability to keep going no matter what – is also reflected in our bodies, in our physical being.'

When people talk about *sisu* and they're trying to describe it, they point to their gut, like it's literally in there – they don't point to their hearts or heads.

So *sisu* is more than simply a psychological mindset or attitude, as it ties into our physical wellbeing.

'We always talk about the brain, but it's also the gut. For example, with nutrition some scientists have been able to treat depression. As an athlete, I can't perform and push myself mentally if I don't take care of my gut. If I eat pizza the night before a run, it will affect my performance,' says Lahti.

Lahti refers to research that indicates the gut produces about 80 per cent (some estimates place it even higher at 90 or 95 per cent) of the serotonin in our entire system.

The neurotransmitter serotonin is associated with brain function, mood and mental wellbeing. Low serotonin levels are associated with depression. Serotonin also helps regulates sleep, memory, learning and libido.

'The mind–body connection, to me, is emerging as the most defining characteristic of this quality. Rather than viewing fortitude as a case of "mind over matter", I propose we view it as "mind with matter",' says Lahti.

Katja Pantzar

Can we increase our *sisu*?

I pose the question to Emilia Lahti: is it possible for a
person to increase their *sisu*?

Lahti doesn't reply with a 'yes' or a 'no', but says:
'Sometimes the most profound things are the most simple
things. If you asked Angela Duckworth how we cultivate grit
she would likely still say, "We don't yet have a complete
answer." However, Duckworth often mentions mindset, the
work of Stanford psychology professor Carol S. Dweck, who
holds that our beliefs are one of the biggest determinants
of our future actions,' explains Lahti.

'It's important to cultivate a mindset that our abilities are
not fixed so that we can grow. That has a huge impact
because our beliefs define our future actions, thus what we
are likely to do. If I don't believe I can leave an abusive
relationship or that I can run a marathon, then I will most
likely not take any action to do those things,' she says.

Browsing Lahti's website emilialahti.com, which has
extensive research and posts on the topic of Finnish
resilience, I find a section of text written by Lahti with what
I'm looking for: '*Sisu* gives rise to what I call an action
mindset; a courageous attitude which contributes to how
we approach challenges. *Sisu* is a way of life to actively

transform the challenges that come our way into opportunities.'

Does that mean that being physically strong or fit can increase your *sisu*?

Lahti is yet to have the data to confirm this but says, 'If I were to hypothesise, I would say that the mind–body connection is one dimension of *sisu*. It's impossible to say where one domain begins and another ends; it's a combination of several different fields. One big example we witness is the power of culture – culture as in an agreed set of values that we as a community hold in high regard. I love that you've lived in Finland long enough to know that it's not cool to give up; it's almost an unspoken code. A certain environment can be conducive to certain ways of behaving, as we align our behaviour because we want to feel that we're accepted in our community,' says Lahti.

Being immersed in a culture of resilience has helped me to transition from being a more passive, cautious and scared-about-trying-new-things type of person to someone who gets out there and takes risks. Those range from the decision to voluntarily leave a secure full-time job to go freelance, to dipping my toes into icy water that first time. I went from 'I can't' and 'I'm too tired' to 'I'll try it', which became 'Wow, this feels great!' and 'If I can do this, what else can I do?' My environment has helped to trigger this shift.

> Being immersed in a culture of resilience has helped me to transition from being a more passive, cautious and scared-about-trying-new-things type of person to someone who gets out there and takes risks.

The origins of *sisu*

According to Finnish-language scholar and expert Maija Länsimäki, the use of the word *sisu* dates back to at least the 1500s, when it appeared in written texts referring to both a personality trait or aspect of someone's nature, and the interior or inside of something. In a dictionary published in 1745 by Finnish writer, bishop and professor Daniel Juslenius, the word *sisucunda* was defined as the location in the human body where strong emotions could be felt.

Earlier notions of 'bad' *sisu* include being too stubborn, having malice and not giving up when it might be the wiser thing to do.

In a contemporary context, having too much *sisu* can mean pushing yourself too hard and not knowing when to stop or ask for help, leading to burnout and other serious health problems.

Lahti stresses that it's important to ensure that *sisu* is used constructively: 'We must also practise self-compassion and be understanding of other people's struggles. The downside of *sisu* is thinking that asking for help is a sign of weakness. This creates a mental landscape where people are very alone with their challenges. No one can bear that. As important as it is to talk about *sisu*, it is important to talk about the quality of our individual and collective *sisu*, as well as to reflect on what it's used for,' she says.

Finland's historic hardships – including the Great Famine of 1867, which left 200,000 people dead, and both World Wars, which took hundreds of thousands of lives and left the country scrambling to rebuild – have contributed to the cultivation of resilience.

At the closing speech of Helsinki's 2012 year as World Design Capital, a noted Finnish design director spoke about what drives the country's design and innovation. Her view was that Finland is a Winter War kind of country; innovation happens when things are tough, not when they're easy and comfortable.

Katja Pantzar

Studies in *sisu*

Dr Barbara Schneider is a professor at Michigan State University at the College of Education and the Department of Sociology. The author of more than fifteen books and over a hundred academic articles, Schneider has played a significant role in developing research methods for the real-time measurements of learning experiences. She is the co-chair of the prestigious Mindset Scholars Network, which has the goal of 'advancing scientific understanding of learning mindsets in order to improve student outcomes'.

In addition to a focus on how social contexts influence the academic performance and wellbeing of adolescents, one of her areas of research interest is the Finnish concept of *sisu*.

I'm first introduced to Schneider's work at the same Helsinki *sisu* seminar where I met Emilia Lahti.

At the event, Schneider, a petite woman with a warm smile, is elected to the Finnish Academy of Science and Letters – she also holds an honorary doctor of philosophy degree from the University of Helsinki. She delivers a brief talk about her research into the role of *sisu* in comparative studies of Finnish and American secondary school students.

The lauded Finnish education system has been closely followed around the world since the first PISA (Programme for International Student Assessment) results in 2001 when Finland, of all the OECD countries, was the highest performer in reading literacy, mathematics and science.

There's a sentence in Schneider's presentation that stays with me: 'We found that when a challenge is higher than your average, in the US kids are more likely to give up, whereas Finnish kids are far less likely to give up; they'll stick with it longer, even when the challenge is very steep.'

~~~

I arrange to interview Schneider by phone to find out more.

We start by talking about the cultural context of *sisu*.

'If you go to the US, things that characterise us include our individualism and our consumerism. Anybody can make it here; all you need is hard work. Whereas in Finland we keep ourselves going in the face of adversity, whatever happens to us. This kind of fortitude is an internalisation of your ability to fortify yourself, to take whatever is given to you,' she says. 'If you look at Finland's history – the famine, the ability to achieve independence, the weather – how people survive is with this kind of inner strength, *sisu*, which isn't the same as grit.'

In order to examine why some students give up and others don't, Schneider and her Finnish colleagues have been studying social and emotional experiences in the educational context for about five years using a programme designed by Google software engineer Robert Evans.

When their data showed that Finnish kids were less likely to give up when faced with a steep challenge, Schneider says it was an important finding for a number of reasons: 'We know that in the US students don't maintain interest and that they're easily bored in school and that we need to develop things that are more challenging for the skill level,' she says. 'Our real interest is to see how we can increase engagement in social, emotional and academic learning in science. Now Finland does amazingly well in science; on the other hand, students don't stay with it after high school – the worry for them and for the world is how we ensure scientific interest among all kids,' she explains.

I ask Schneider why she's interested in *sisu*.

'We are faced with the fact that our weather is not stable; our earth is not a stable place, which has real implications for global warming. We will need to rely on these younger people to experiment and change things and to be adaptable to the future that we're likely to have. We're very interested to understand how we can create a more entrepreneurial state among young people, have them understand more about science, technology, modelling – the kinds of skill sets that they're going to need to keep this planet alive and healthy.'

Can *sisu* be taught?

Schneider replies that she's not sure. 'These are things that happen to people in the context of living some place and having a national identity. It's more a kind of orientation to life. However, I do think that issues like persistence, not giving up in the face of a challenge, can be taught.

'From my perspective, *sisu* is one of the reasons why Finland is so successful on PISA tests and such a successful nation given the fact they're such a small group; that and how heavily they invest in their humans. That's what they do – they invest heavily in education and society,' she says.

Issues like persistence, not giving up in the face of a challenge, can be taught.

Around the same time, I meet another American professor, Douglas, who is a scholar of Greek classics and spending a year in Helsinki. On the dock where I go for my daily dips, he is one of the many year-round swimmers I chat with.

Always interested in an outsider's opinion, I ask him what he thinks *sisu* is.

'*Sisu* requires a positive exercise of will; it's a muscle you exercise,' he says definitively, affirming what I've also come to think.

A *sisu* mindset

- Sisu *is an ancient Finnish construct relating to mental toughness, fortitude and resilience.*
- *It's the ability to endure significant stress, while taking action against seemingly impossible odds.*

'*Sisu* gives rise to what I call an action mindset; a courageous attitude which contributes to how we approach challenges. *Sisu* is a way of life to actively transform the challenges that come our way into opportunities.'

Sisu *expert Emilia Lahti*

- *Instead of 'I can't' or 'I won't' how about 'How can I?'*
- *Good physical health and wellbeing can help to build up* sisu.

CHAPTER 3

Cold-water cure: can winter swimming alleviate the symptoms of depression, stress and fatigue?

The first time I try winter swimming falls on Valentine's Day, which is largely celebrated in Finland as a day of friendship rather than romantic love as in some other parts of the world.

In hindsight, given how I quickly I fall in love with the practice and the many friends and acquaintances I make through it, it's seems fitting that my first foray into chilly waters takes place on a day marked on the calendar by endearment.

The opportunity to try it out comes in the form of a serendipitous invitation when I meet a group of enthusiastic winter swimmers at my friend Tiina's dinner party one evening.

Which is how I find myself wearing nothing but a bathing suit and a wool hat and standing outside on a dock on a frosty dark February evening beside Riikka, one of the enthusiastic winter swimmers I met at the dinner party. A very youthful-looking mother of three adult children, who also runs her own business, Riikka looks more like a teenager than a middle-ager.

As an arctic wind blows, I shiver.

~~~~~

Before we set out, Riikka gave me a few pointers, and offered to lend me her rubber swimming gloves and shoes, as the anti-slip gravel sprinkled on the ice during the slippery winter months can be painful to walk on barefoot, and extremities such as hands and feet are very sensitive to the extreme cold. Riikka, like most of the other swimmers, wears a wool hat to keep warm and it's on her advice that I'm also wearing one.

I've scanned the general safety rules posted on the wall of the changing rooms: one should not go winter swimming after consuming alcohol, if sick with fever, flu or suffering from other illnesses such as a heart condition, high blood pressure or asthma, without first consulting a doctor. Diving into the water is cautioned against – one should gradually lower oneself into the water so that the body can get acclimatised to the cold water. And going with a friend is recommended.

Riikka goes in first and shows me how she gradually lowers herself into the water before swimming a small loop. This seems incredibly brave to me and I'm already anticipating my turn with a sense of dread, telling myself over and over, 'This is a ridiculous thing to be doing!'

When it's my turn, I slowly lower myself into the frigid water, gasping for breath as my eyes widen because the water (2 degrees Celsius) is so shockingly and painfully cold. I'm only able to lower myself down the ladder a few notches, so that the unbearably cold water is up to my chest, before I quickly clamber back up onto the dock.

My first instinct is to run back to the sauna building in search of warmth. But then, quite suddenly, all the now numb parts of my body that were immersed in the water start to tingle and the pain of the cold is replaced by a warm glow. It's as though I've had a massage or taken a strong painkiller, the effects of which have just kicked in.

> **Suddenly, all the now numb parts of my body that were immersed in the water start to tingle and the pain of the cold is replaced by a warm glow.**

We head back for a shower followed by a hot sauna, which feels absolutely divine after the icy water. As Riikka ladles water over the rocks in the sauna, I psych myself up for another quick dip before we go because I'm feeling quite fantastic.

That night I sleep better than I have in ages. It's as though my stress and tiredness have been replaced by a contented calm, which is a rare feeling for me.

The art of an icy dip

Many of the winter swimming clubs in Finland have waiting lists, but I'm in luck: it turns out that Riikka's club, which is just a few blocks from where I live at the time with my husband and son, is accepting new members.

I'm able to join immediately for an annual fee of about 100 euros. This means that between the hours of 6 a.m. and 10.30 p.m. seven days a week during the season, which runs from November to the end of March, I have access to the dock, as well as to the changing rooms and showers, and sauna.

I start by going a few evenings a week, and it takes one full season before I'm actually able to get into the water and swim a few breaststrokes (I've never been a particularly good swimmer). That first season consists largely of me having one quick dip in which I barely immerse my shoulders in the water before shrieking (internally) and getting out and heading to the sauna to warm up before having a second, slightly longer dip.

But by the third season, I'm able to go straight into the water the first time and complete a small thirty-second or so swim. As my stamina and *sisu* grow, I develop a better resistance to the cold and it no longer feels so painful during those first few seconds of immersion. There's also a no-pain no-gain mindset that I adopt, for I know that those initial seconds of extreme discomfort will be rewarded by a fantastic feeling of bliss.

My new hobby sets in motion a series of changes.

The rush of endorphins and the positive nature of socialising with people who feel great do wonders for my mood, especially after a busy day in a newsroom or rushing to meet a deadline.

In the evening, when I have that 'I need a drink!' feeling after a stressful day, I find myself going for a quick dip instead of reaching for a bottle.

The euphoric feeling that I have post-dip reminds me of the buzz that I used to get from drinking a few glasses of wine (or more) in an attempt to feel better and to rid myself of, well, myself and my feelings of anxiety. But my cold-water buzz has none of the unpleasant side effects of alcohol, such as poor sleep and a tired, sluggish feeling the next day. I quickly realise that my cold-water cure provides a much purer and stronger boost than a glass of wine or two.

I have long had a conflicted relationship with alcohol, which is widely known to be a depressant and generally not the recommended beverage of choice for those prone to feeling down. I have, of course, been fully aware of this and am the proud owner of at least twenty years' worth of diaries and notebooks filled with self-improvement resolution lists featuring one item that repeatedly and (imploringly) shows up: 'Drink less!'

But it's not until I discover this icy form of shock therapy that provides relief from almost all that ails my mind and body that I realise how much of my drinking has been an attempt to improve my mood.

Winter swimming hasn't turned me into a teetotaller – I still enjoy a glass or two of wine or champagne on a special occasion – but alcohol is no longer my go-to fix.

It's also a very simple equation: the less I drink the better I feel and the happier I am. But it's taken me almost a lifetime to arrive at this place.

A remedy for a range of ailments

My cold dips also provide a natural remedy for many other ailments, from tiredness and stress, to neck and muscle tension due to spending too many hours hunched over a keyboard. Instead of reaching for a painkiller, I start experimenting with going for a dip first. In many instances, it does the trick and my pain subsides.

I start to consider the sea my pharmacy, for it seems that a great many pains and problems get left in the water, a sentiment my fellow cold-water swimmers share.

My cold dips also provide a natural remedy for many other ailments, from tiredness and stress, to neck and muscle tension.

My new practice also has a meditative effect: it forces me to be present in the moment, a valuable skill for someone who has a habit of ruminating, a hallmark of depression and anxiety. In addition to the positive physiological effects of alternating hot (sauna) and cold (swim), which relax both muscles and mind, the icy water brings me into the moment. It cuts into whatever track is spinning in my mind – 'must do this, must do that, did I do the right thing?' – and forces me to be present, to touch, feel, hear, see and even taste the current moment.

That break, even if it's only for thirty seconds in the water, acts like a reset button. And the temporary escape makes everything seem much more manageable. It refocuses my view from everything that seems wrong with the world to everything that is right.

In addition to providing a remedy for a range of ailments, my cold therapy helps to alleviate the low-grade level of pain that I often feel, which is a symptom of depression. It is not a specific ache, but a sluggish, lethargic feeling that makes it difficult to find the motivation to do things. When I discover that this fatigue-y feeling is neatly cut by an icy dip and replaced by a fabulous omnipotent energy, I realise I have an easy solution for managing my weariness.

And I am not alone. As I get to know the many dynamic winter swimmers, who range in age from their teens to their eighties, all of whom practise daily acts of *sisu* through winter swimming, I hear their stories about why they come to *avanto*, as it's called in Finnish, and what benefits they get from it.

It forces me to be present in the moment.

Though I also chat with the men on the dock at the winter swimming club, it's the women I get to know better as we share the changing room and the sauna where we talk.

There are the spry seventy- and eighty-year-olds in their brightly coloured swimsuits and caps with a sparkle in their eyes, who come early each morning for a quick dip *sans* sauna and tell me, 'The water keeps muscle aches at bay,' adding that it helps them 'to deal with insomnia and sleep through the night'. Many swimmers say that they don't fully wake up, especially during the dark winter months, until they've had their dip. Several say it keeps their mood buoyant. Menopausal women tell me they use the water to help them cool down during hot flushes.

There are just as many reasons as there are swimmers; some simply use the cold-water therapy to reduce stress and as a coping mechanism for dealing with the challenges of modern life: so much to do and so little time, which seems to be a universal dilemma.

Women who are juggling busy careers with taking care of children and elderly parents tell me that this is their saviour, the thing that gives them a much-needed break from everything, and reinvigorates them.

I also hear women tell me that the seawater is good for their skin – if they have sensitive skin or eczema, the brackish Baltic helps with the itchiness. It's like nature's equivalent to soaking in an Epsom salt bath.

Although we swim in the sea almost in the centre of Helsinki, one of the most traditional forms of winter swimming or *avanto* is going for a dip in a hole or square drilled into the ice of a frozen lake. Finland, which is known as the country of a thousand lakes, actually has 187,888 lakes.

Though estimates place the number of active winter swimmers in Finland in the hundreds of thousands, not everyone is running around jumping into cold water. Some of the locals in our neighbourhood out for a walk stop and shake their heads and express their amazement at what they perceive to be our braveness – or foolishness for that matter.

And then there are the smartphone- and camera-toting tourists, who come by to snap a photo or two of what they see to be an exotic and extreme activity. They watch with amazement as we go into the water – and we entertain ourselves by coming up with a range of answers to the inevitable question: 'Is the water cold?'

'No, actually this part of the sea is heated for us especially by the city,' we reply, giggling as we walk back to the changing rooms and slip out of sight.

Historical roots

Using cold water for health and wellness has a long history in many parts of the world. The Romans had a *frigidarium*, a cold bath used for cooling off after a warm *tepidarium* or hot *caldarium* bath.

Winter swimming is practised in Russia, China, the Baltics, and some of the other Nordic countries, including Sweden. It also appears to be gaining popularity in parts of North America, though the emphasis is on swimming distances rather than simply taking quick dips. In the UK, cold-water swimming and wild swimming are growing massively in popularity, particularly among women, with a raft of websites and books on the topic. Sports therapy has long utilised ice baths to relieve sore muscles.

In Finland, written accounts of winter swimming date back to the 1600s and 1700s when travel reports by foreign visitors chronicled the curiosities they encountered, according to a Finnish-language guide on the topic. Titled *Hyinen Hurmio*, which roughly translates to 'Glacial Ecstasy', the book, published in the year 2000, was written by Taina Kinnunen, Pasi Heikura and Pirkko Huttunen, a now retired biochemist and docent of thermo biology, whose work is often cited in the Finnish media on the *avanto* topic.

Using cold water for health and wellness has a long history in many parts of the world.

According to the book, winter swimming was a way to cool down after having a hot sauna; another popular way to cool off post-sauna during the winter months was (and continues to be) rolling in the snow.

The volume is one of the few I find that chronicles the Finnish history of ice swimming and contains research on the physiological, and other, effects of the practice.

'Studies have shown that winter swimming affects people in many different ways. For a lot of people it relieves stress, as the cold releases stress hormones. Continuous exposure to cold water naturally improves the tolerance to cold water and to the cold in general. As the body is toughened against the cold, its immunity is also improved. Winter swimming affects both the body's immune and antioxidant systems, which may help the body to endure various external strains. When swimming is continued it will most likely lower blood pressure. The effects of winter swimming and other forms of cryotherapy in treating such conditions as rheumatism have also been studied and the results have been encouraging. In Finland, cryotherapy is used for pain relief and to treat arthritis. Results from elsewhere have shown it also to be very effective in improving the respiration of people suffering from asthma.'

Cold power

I've heard plenty of anecdotes about the benefits of winter swimming, but I'm interested to know whether there's research to back it up.

My quest to better understand why winter swimming does such wonders leads me to one of the country's top experts on the effects of cold, professor Hannu Rintamäki, who has devoted his forty-year career to studying, among other things, the effects of Arctic weather on the human body from an occupational and wellbeing perspective.

I initially speak with Rintamäki by phone to find out more about the measurable effects of cold-water immersion on the human body.

'A dip of about thirty seconds to one minute in water that's on average about 4 degrees Celsius during the winter months causes what's known as a "hormone storm", as many of the so-called happy hormones are pushed into action,' Rintamäki explains.

'The happy hormones include endorphins, the body's natural pain killers, serotonin [widely thought to maintain mood balance], dopamine [the neurotransmitter that helps control the brain's reward and pleasure centres and also helps to regulate movement and emotional response], and oxytocin [also known as the love hormone],' he says.

Which provides a concise explanation for the positive effects I've experienced.

'In addition, blood circulation is enhanced, calories are burned and the immune system gets a boost. It's very effective given that an average dip is one minute; it's a minute very well spent for its multitude of benefits,' he says, adding, 'The heart rate accelerates and after the rush of endorphins, there's a peaceful feeling.'

During our conversation it turns out that Rintamäki carried out laboratory tests on winter swimmers with professor and *Glacial Ecstasy* co-author Pirkko Huttunen in the late 1990s.

As I'm interested to see the lab and find out more, I travel to the northern town of Oulu where professor Rintamäki is based at both the Finnish Institute of Occupational Health and the University of Oulu.

Tucked just below the Arctic Circle, Oulu has the feeling of a friendly small town, where the pace of life is slower and more laid back than in the capital 600 kilometres away.

Given my newfound fascination and interest in the power of the cold, it seems that Finland's fourth largest city is a good place to be. The University of Oulu's expert focus is Arctic know-how, which is about thriving in a frosty climate.

Oulu's other claims to fame include holding the title of Winter Cycling Capital of the World. The city also hosts the annual Polar Bear Pitch, an event that draws participants from around the globe to give their entrepreneurial pitch while standing waist deep in water in an ice hole carved into the Baltic Sea. Pitches by participants trying to secure backing or seed money for their ideas are short and sweet out of frigid necessity.

I meet Rintamäki, a trim-looking sixty-something with an affable smile and a friendly manner, in the foyer of a modern low-rise building which houses his office and lab. I later discover he cycles all year round like many of his fellow Oulu-ites.

Rintamäki takes me on a tour of the lab that holds all manner of measuring machines. In addition to a wind tunnel where people, outdoor safety clothing and equipment can be tested in extreme weather conditions, he shows me the lab's small cold-water pool where he and his colleagues carried out experiments to measure the physiological effects of cold dips on the human body.

One of the key pieces of feedback they received from participants, he says, was that the lab environment was problematic.

'It's not just the act of dipping into water; winter swimming is as much about the connection with nature and the elements, especially for city dwellers who may not have daily contact with the outdoors. For example, consider someone who travels by car to an office that is artificially lit and then spends most of the day online in front of a computer,' he says.

'Walking to the water is part of the experience – you feel the air on your skin, you see the water and the scenery, you are present outdoors in a natural way. You receive sensory feedback, which is something that city dwellers don't necessarily get. Our sensory system was developed with nature in mind. Living in a type of virtual reality without a connection to earth is not good for human beings,' he explains.

The sensory feedback link is key for me because it feels as though for many years I unknowingly neglected my connection to nature. It was not for lack of opportunity – Canada is full of nature – but living in congested cities I didn't appreciate the importance of trying to incorporate daily doses of nature into my life.

My parents took me out into the woods of Greater Vancouver as a child, and as a teenager I attended a high-school outdoor wilderness programme. But in my

urban adult life, nature – whether woods, lake or beach
– was often just a temporary destination at the end of a
car trip.

Another point that Rintamäki highlights, which I've heard
from many of my fellow swimmers, is that winter swimming
is about self-care. It's about taking the initiative and that
'badass' feeling that comes from doing something difficult.
Sisu management, if you will.

Like those books and magazines that opened up a
whole new world to me as a child and adolescent, winter
swimming opens up a whole new way of thinking: if I can
do this, what else can I do?

Both experts and lay people have identified cold-water
cures for depression.

A 2007 research paper by professor Nikolai Shevchuk,
then a researcher and molecular biologist at Virginia
Commonwealth University School of Medicine, set out to
study the hypothesis that depression may be caused by the
convergence of two factors:

'(A) A lifestyle that lacks certain physiological stressors
that have been experienced by primates through millions

of years of evolution, such as brief changes in body temperature (e.g. a cold swim), and this lack of 'thermal exercise' may cause inadequate functioning of the brain. (B) Genetic makeup that predisposes an individual to be affected by the above condition more seriously than other people.'

Though I can also relate to the genetic element, it is the first point that I particularly identify with. It took me a long time to realise that I might *benefit* from physiological stressors. Shevchuk's research experiment used adapted cold showers for a set period of time – a great option for people who don't want to or can't take an icy swim.

According to Shevchuk's abstract: 'Exposure to cold is known to activate the sympathetic nervous system and increase the blood level of beta-endorphin and noradrenaline and to increase synaptic release of noradrenaline in the brain as well. Additionally, due to the high density of cold receptors in the skin, a cold shower is expected to send an overwhelming amount of electrical impulses from peripheral nerve endings to the brain, which could result in an anti-depressive effect.'

Though at the end of his study Shevchuk concluded that further research was needed, it is interesting that the tests indicated that cold hydrotherapy had the potential to relieve depressive symptoms.

Now that I've discovered using cold water as a positive physiological stressor, I've experimented with taking cold showers of fifteen to thirty seconds when I don't have access to a natural body of cold water. Though my experience is that it's not quite the same, I do get some benefits. When I emerge from a cool shower my whole body tingles and then feels reinvigorated. Shivering dissipates and a sense of calm follows, which is especially useful if I'm stressed and can't sleep.

Sisu expert Emilia Lahti tells me that she has used cold showers as a mental strength-building technique.

'I'm someone who absolutely hates cold water, but I have this inbuilt system that seeks to challenge myself. If something sounds hard, I want to try it,' says Lahti. 'The cold triggers your survival mechanism – deep breaths in, and get out of there! But by day five, I got used to it and could stay in long enough to wash my hair. That just tells us about the adaptability of our limits and exceeding them. That's why I would say that physical activity is the thing to do when it comes to what underlies *sisu*.'

I also discuss using cold water to treat depression with my friend Riikka, the woman who first took me winter swimming, who also happens to be a psychotherapist.

Speaking in her professional capacity Riikka Toivanen says she would be interested to see more research into winter swimming and its possible benefits in helping to treat those who suffer from depression.

'The challenge is, of course, that when a person is depressed, it's so much harder for them to get up and do things. Their *sisu* is the first thing to go. But winter swimming is a direct and immediate route to being in the moment – there's no other option. And when someone gets that powerful, great feeling when they come out of the water, it can be such a definitive experience – *Hey, life can be like this!*' she says.

I tell her that I have long considered the cold water as a kind of natural shock therapy.

To which Riikka (like professor Rintamäki) draws parallels: 'In lieu of electric shock, cold-water shock is much healthier and has fewer negative side effects,' she says.

As the cryotherapy craze sweeps the world, with people paying good money to be placed in tanks that blasts nitrogen-chilled air at much colder temperatures than 1 or 2 degrees Celsius, it strikes me that many of the benefits people credit to cryotherapy are the same ones that my polar pastime provides.

Winter swimming to treat other conditions

In my search for people who use winter swimming to treat other medical and health-related conditions, I meet up with the multi-talented Päivi Pälvimäki, who teaches winter swimming courses. Her love of the water makes her the perfect aquatic ambassador. One of the main reasons she is a winter swimming instructor is because she 'wants to share the joy and happiness *avanto* gives to people'.

We meet at Allas Sea Pool, a floating outdoor swimming pool complex nestled in Helsinki's central harbour, with an unparalleled view of the historic buildings near the waterfront which represent a range of architectural styles from neo-classical to functionalism. The complex is a great example of community spirit. With heated pools and a cold-water sea pool, saunas and an outdoor gym, it was partially built using crowd-funding.

Formerly a university art lecturer, Pälvimäki says 'the swimming took over' about six years ago and became her full-time career.

She partnered up with Finnish marathon swimmer Tuomas Kaario, who swam over the Gulf of Finland and was the first Finn to swim across both the English Channel and the Strait of Gibraltar. The duo started Finland's first open-water swimming association in 2015.

Her love of polar dips is also personal – she has used the practice to recover from two surgeries for ruptured discs.

'I've had two back operations in the last five years – my disc broke in the same spot here,' she says, pointing to her lower spine. 'I noticed the cold water really helped me to recover; it lowered the inflammation around the disc and the muscles. It helped me get back into life when I was feeling a bit down following surgery and aided in the recovery process,' she says.

As I have seen close-up with friends and family members how debilitating back operations for slipped discs can be, I ask whether there were any risks associated with cold-water swimming post-surgery.

'I was really careful with every movement. But I've worked up to swimming again, not just going for a dip, and it doesn't hurt. I believe it makes me stronger,' she replies.

Pälvimäki, like many Finns, tells me that she learned to swim at the family summer cottage as a child. Indeed, swimming seems to be a national pastime and I find statistics to back that up: according to a recent survey by the Finnish Swimming Teaching and Lifesaving Federation, 72 per cent of twelve-year-olds have the ability to swim.

I ask her how many winter swimmers there are in the country.

'The popularity of winter swimming is growing; many clubs have waiting lists for accepting new members. Results from the last survey in 2010 by the Outdoor Association found that 150,000 people were active swimmers and 500,000 were occasional ones,' she says.

I'm curious to see how she instructs, so Pälvimäki gives me a live demo in the sea pool, which is a refreshing 10 degrees Celsius on this early spring day in May.

'My main goal is to encourage participants and to provide a safe atmosphere. First-timers can look into my eyes when they initially get into the water. Before they do, I instruct them on how to breathe in and out so as not to hyperventilate from the shock of the cold. Then I say, try to relax and listen to your body. Come up whenever you want. If it's just a dip at first, that's good, it's enough.'

She also discusses specific conditions such as Raynaud's disease that might prevent people from partaking and lets participants know about neoprene socks and gloves that

are useful, since hands and feet are especially susceptible
to the cold.

'I recommend wearing a hat or a cap, and drinking warm
tea, juice or water, because the temperature change can
take its toll: when you're cold you don't know if you're
dehydrated. I also suggest swimming in lakes or the sea
during the summer and then continuing in the fall, so
acclimatisation comes gradually with nature,' she adds.

When our demo wraps up, she asks in true Finnish style,
'Shall we go for a sauna?'

The benefits of winter swimming

'A dip of about thirty seconds to one minute in water that's on average about four degrees Celsius during the winter months causes what's known as a "hormone storm", as many of the so-called happy hormones are pushed into action.'

Research professor Hannu Rintamäki

The happy hormones include endorphins, the body's natural pain killers, serotonin [widely thought to maintain mood balance], dopamine [the neurotransmitter that helps control the brain's reward and pleasure centres and also helps to regulate movement and emotional response], and oxytocin [also known as the love hormone].

- *Provides stress relief*
- *Continuous exposure to cold water improves cold tolerance in general*
- *It improves immunity*
- *It provides pain relief*
- *It's a natural stimulant when feeling tired*

You can recreate some of the conditions of winter swimming at home:

- *A cold shower can carry some of the same invigorating benefits as a dip in icy waters.*
- *Start with a few seconds of cold and progress to a longer stretch each day.*
- *Even a thirty-second or one-minute cold shower can be invigorating.*
- *Moderation is key: if you try to go for five minutes immediately, it will likely put you off the whole process.*
- *Follow up with a warm shower.*

CHAPTER 4

Soul of the sauna: sweat your way to better health

~~~

A woman is at her most beautiful after a sauna, according to a popular Finnish saying. Though the healthy red-cheeked glow that comes from a good sauna session is definitely part of its steamy allure, I've started to interpret the expression in a more holistic way: the inner sense of calm and bliss that follows a detoxifying and relaxing steam.

My winter swimming expert Päivi Pälvimäki and I are sitting in the women's sauna of the Allas Sea Pool after we've finished our interview.

Through the sauna window there's a view to the main Helsinki harbour where the large cruise ships that ply the waters between Stockholm, Tallinn and the Finnish capital come to dock. Smaller ferries sailing to the nearby fortress island of Suomenlinna pass by almost in front of us.

As we chat, I ladle water from a bucket to create *löyly*, the hot steam that rises when the water hits the sauna stove's rocks. I marvel over the fact that Päivi and I are sitting here post-interview swim – talking about open-water swimming, nature and saunas – naked, as per sauna etiquette.

Yet we only just met for the first time today. Neither of us has a stitch of clothing on, but I don't feel the least bit uncomfortable.

Growing up, I was uneasy with the idea of the sauna and feigned excuses in order to avoid it. On trips and stays in Finland, especially as a teenager, the idea of sitting in a steamy room naked with my female relatives or friends filled me with real anxiety. Getting undressed in front of other people was simply inconceivable – I was uncomfortable enough with my own body, so the idea of public nudity was preposterous to me.

Gradually, over the years of living in Finland I have found a zone where I feel perfectly comfortable in the raw. The sauna is such a quintessential part of life and social get-togethers that not having a sauna would be akin to refusing to eat with everyone at a dinner party.

During the early years I remember going with my then-boyfriend, the man who would later became my husband, to spend the midsummer weekend at a cottage in Punkaharju, a pine-filled esker ridge surrounded by large lakes in the pristine nature of Eastern Finland.

Along with the traditional midsummer's eve bonfire and copious amounts of drinking to celebrate the day when the sun doesn't set, one of the traditions for this group of twenty or so friends was to enjoy a traditional smoke sauna – naked.

Now the norm is for men and women to sauna separately, or to wear swimsuits if in mixed company. My first instinct at the time was to hide behind a towel or a bathing suit. But as everyone else was *sans* swimsuits, a towel or bathing suit would have only attracted more attention.

As with many aspects of life in the Nordics, the focus here was on the group, not the individual. We instead of me. The intention was to have a traditional smoke sauna together; no one cared about how anybody looked naked, whether I thought my breasts were too small, or about any other body-image issues I might have had, for that matter. In the event it was actually incredibly liberating and an effective way to hone my *sisu* by mustering up the courage to do something that felt foreign and uncomfortable. Getting comfortable with being naked requires a sort of sauna *sisu* for the uninitiated.

An ancient tradition

The word 'sauna' is the best known of the few Finnish-language words to make it into the English-language dictionary.

According to the Finnish Sauna Society, the sauna tradition has continued unbroken for 2,000 years.

There are variations of the steam bath found around the world ranging from the Russian *banja* to the Japanese *furo* and the sweat lodges of the First Nations in North America.

As for the Finnish sauna, some sources date the original smoke sauna – one without a chimney that's heated up for several hours before the smoke is let out for the sauna-goers to come in and enjoy the experience – as being up to 10,000 years old.

In older times, saunas were considered so important that they were often built before the family house. Once considered the most sterile place to deliver a baby, saunas were also where the deceased were prepared for their final journey.

Traditional wood-burning saunas are often found at cottages or places seriously devoted to a good steam, such as the members-only Finnish Sauna Society on the island of Lauttasaari in Helsinki. Electric saunas are more common in houses and apartment buildings, and public swimming pools and gyms.

In older times, saunas were considered so important that they were often built before the family house.

For many aficionados, an essential part of the steam-bath ritual includes the sauna whisk (*vihta*) made from soaked birch leaves that are used to gently 'whisk' either yourself or someone else. Now if that sounds odd, it's not. Think of it as the Finnish version of the kind of tapping or pounding that occurs in certain types of massages for relaxation. Not only does it feel good, it fills the air with a natural birch scent and is thought to relieve muscle tension and improve circulation.

Above all, the sauna is a place for cleansing mind and body.

While some of the older sauna etiquette guidelines are quite strict – one should behave as in a church, with no loud talking, swearing, or speaking of politics allowed – in my experience people discuss all manner of topics in the modern-day sauna.

In a country of 5.5 million people, it's estimated that there are about 3.3 million saunas, which makes Finland a country of sauna experts.

I later message Päivi Pälvimäki to ask her what the Finnish steam bath means to her.

'It's a very traditional, almost holy place: I can relate to previous generations, the time when women gave birth in the sauna, and prepared the dead in the sauna before taking them to the grave for burial,' she replies.

It's also a place for solitude, she says. 'I like to go to the sauna alone. It's a kind of retreat, to not have to talk to anyone, to lie down, have my own rhythm with *löyly* and listen to my body.'

In a country of 5.5 million people, it's estimated that there are about 3.3 million saunas

Health benefits

Pälvimäki shares something that a great many people have told me: 'Especially in the wintertime the sauna is like the sun: it ignites your inner light and warms you on cold and dark winter days.'

Whatever the weather, when you emerge from a steamy session in the sauna, which is typically heated to temperatures between 70 to 100 degrees Celsius, you feel warm and happy inside.

Päivi says that she also uses the sauna for health reasons.

'My back muscles are very sensitive to stress. The sauna relaxes both muscles and thoughts. It reduces stress to lower blood pressure, which is really good for me because there's a risk of high blood pressure in our family. I haven't had to take blood pressure medication and I think it's owing to this,' she says, referring to the sauna.

According to the revered Finnish Sauna Society, the sauna's health benefits include:

- soothing and relaxing tired muscles
- relieving tension and mental and physical fatigue
- improving circulation
- lowering blood pressure

- affecting better and more restful sleep
- increasing resistance to illness
- maintaining clear and healthy skin, and removing toxins and impurities.

The Society cites Finnish and German studies, which indicate that regular sauna sessions can decrease the chances of catching a cold or flu by 30 per cent.

A 2017 study of middle-aged Finnish men carried out by the Institute of Public Health and Clinical Nutrition at the University of Eastern Finland and the School of Clinical Sciences, University of Bristol, in the UK, found that moderate to frequent sauna bathing was associated with lowered risks of dementia and Alzheimer's disease.

There are a number of popular Finnish proverbs praising the health qualities of a good steam, including: 'If sauna, liquor or tar don't help, the disease is probably fatal.' Wood tar (*terva*) extracted from birch trees (*the* Finnish tree) is used to treat everything from digestion to skin problems.

Reportedly, Finnish author F. E. Sillanpää, who was awarded the Nobel Prize in 1939 for his novel *The Maid Silja*, used the sauna to relieve depression and fatigue following long writing sessions.

Sauna spirit

Another brilliant aspect of the sauna is that it's a great equaliser. As everyone is naked, it's a stripped-down playing field, so to speak. In the public and private saunas that dot the country, people chat to one another without necessarily knowing each other's names, professions or any other personal details. Whether the person sitting next to you owns a Lada or a BMW, a Rolex or a Timex, is irrelevant. All walks of life sit together on the wooden benches.

And at a time when many people are glued to their mobile devices, it's a natural digital detox zone; phones aren't allowed and don't belong in the hot steam.

My son, like so many children in Finland, is growing up going to public saunas and swimming pools. As it's mandatory to shower before taking a sauna, young children see people of all ages naked before they step into the sauna. A young boy will go to the women's showers and sauna with his mum and see girls and women naked. As such, from an early age children know that boys and girls have different body parts and it's absolutely not a big deal.

I'm sure that this teaches children to be more comfortable with their bodies because they're not made to feel that they should cover them up or be ashamed of them.

It also means that everyone grows up seeing all types of bodies and learns that that is the norm, not the super-styled, airbrushed images of 'perfect' bodies we see in magazines or on social media.

~

Many people associate the ideal sauna with a lakeside country cottage. It's a tradition to this day that Finns often spend several weeks relaxing in the countryside during the summer holidays. But there is also a vibrant urban public sauna culture in cities throughout the country.

Helsinki Sauna Day celebrates the quintessential Finnish steam bath. Founded by Jaakko Blomberg, an urban activist and producer, who has become a poster boy for the city's collaborative community spirit, Sauna Day became an instant hit with more than fifty private and public saunas opening their doors when the event was held for the first time in March 2016.

I meet Blomberg, a tall young man in his early thirties with long blond hair pulled back into a ponytail, in the hipster neighbourhood of Kallio.

Over a vegetarian lunch Blomberg tells me that there were several reasons for starting up Sauna Day.

'We have a very busy and communal summer that's relatively short, and then what? That's why the event takes place in March and October during the colder times of the year when people don't necessarily encounter one another as easily.'

Another reason for the event was the communal aspect.

'Sauna breaks social norms and everyone chats with everyone,' he says, adding that some festival-goers visited and spent time in eighteen saunas in one day.

'A Finn is totally different in the sauna,' says Blomberg. 'I recently spoke with a Spaniard who said one of the only ways to have the opportunity to talk with a Finn is to take your clothes off and go and sit next to them!'

It's true, there are several cultural stereotypes about Finns, who are known to be reserved, quiet and perhaps not the smiliest, small-talkiest people around. This mirrors a self-contained reticence or introversion that I've encountered in other parts of northern Europe.

I ask Blomberg what sauna means to him.

'It's a social meeting place and a place for relaxation. It's also a tradition: when I was growing up, like many Finns we had a family sauna every Saturday,' he says.

'People also talk about important issues in the sauna. I ran into a friend and during our conversation it became evident that some time had passed since I had split up with my previous girlfriend. When the subject came up, my friend said, "Why didn't you tell me?" I thought about it for a moment and replied: "I haven't had a chance – we haven't been to the sauna together!" '

~~~~

In addition to newer events such as Sauna Day, there's a flourishing public sauna scene in Helsinki with a long history that includes old-school public saunas such as Arla and Kotiharjun Sauna that have been operating since the 1920s. Part of the experience is sitting outdoors post-steam and chatting with fellow sauna-goers while enjoying a beer or two.

In recent years, several new public saunas have joined the fray, including Allas Sea Pool and Löyly, a wooden design masterpiece that sits on an uncrowded stretch of the city's southern shorefront. The architecturally award-winning structure is shaped like a boulder, with its sharp lines visible from afar. With a traditional smoke sauna and two wood-burning saunas, Löyly has steps and a ladder to the sea for a refreshing dip all year round and therefore the option for first-timers to test out some icy *sisu* in the waters of the Baltic.

One of the liveliest and most affordable – it's free – public saunas in the city is Sompasauna, a makeshift self-service wood-burning sauna that's maintained by everyone who brings firewood and water. The atmosphere is a bit like going to a house party, as Sompasauna is located on an otherwise abandoned shoreline strip of Helsinki. To me, it's the perfect example of Nordic DIY *sisu* and community spirit: there's no manager or caretaker, it's simply based on trust and the idea that everyone will respect and take care of it.

~

Through my winter swimming practice I spend more time in the sauna, especially in the evenings, and come to consider it a modern-day version of an ancient campfire, as we sit on the wooden benches gathered around the heated stove and tell stories or discuss the issues of the day.

There's the psychological letting off steam, as we chat about the world, work and our spouses.

The sauna's social aspect intrigues me; until recently I'd focused solely on its health benefits.

By now, well over a decade into my life in Finland, I have pretty much gone native, so to speak. My spoken Finnish is good enough that people often think I'm a Finn (I do have a Finnish passport) with a bit of an accent who perhaps smiles and talks to strangers more than the locals, but that's thanks to my Canadian upbringing.

The language that I think in is English, not Finnish, and most of my work is in English. Nevertheless, I have spent years reading Finnish newspapers and other texts in an effort to brush up on my spoken and written Finnish, which was very basic when I first arrived.

The reality is that I'm an outsider; I don't always catch cultural and historical references. As such, I'm drawn to other foreigners and I'm interested in their take on Finnish pastimes.

I initially arrange to meet my fellow winter swimmer Douglas, the visiting Greek classics scholar and professor, to chat further about winter swimming, which he neatly refers to as 'a cool entrée into Finnish society'.

But as we talk over coffee one morning in our neighbourhood, I realise that what he has to say about the sauna offers insights I hadn't considered.

'Finland is hard to get into socially,' he says. Which is true. Although an overwhelming majority of people speak good English, if you don't speak Finnish you're not privy to what's going on in the same way.

'The sauna has been a fantastic social tool,' says Douglas. 'When people take off their clothes it changes things. Because I'm a member of the winter swimming club, I'm participating in and am part of the local culture. How does someone new to Finland meet people? I would say that I've made fifteen to twenty friends through this pastime. When I'm in the sauna there's a very interesting cross section of society.'

I understand that there's little need to learn Finnish if you're only visiting. Finnish also holds a reputation of being a hard language to learn. It belongs to the Finno–Ugric group and its closest relations are Hungarian and Estonian. There are numerous grammatical cases, an absence of articles such as 'a' and 'the', and it's totally genderless – there is no 'he' or 'she' – instead *hän* refers to men and women, another nod to equality. It's also completely phonetic: what you see is what you sound.

But I do know Canadians, Americans, Italians, Brits, Russians, Trinidadians and Indians living in Finland who have learned Finnish, illustrating that it's not totally impossible to learn the language.

As we talk, I also find Douglas's take on winter swimming fresh.

'My view is heterodox,' he says. 'You pick up the story about the great health benefits, how long you should be in the water – the consensus seems to be thirty seconds – and this is the story Finns have told themselves, a narrative created to justify the pastime.'

'Is it true?' he asks. 'If it makes you feel good, it doesn't matter. It's improved my wellbeing – otherwise I would be isolated. I'm part of something that's very important in Finnish society. It's social bonding, talking, and doing tough things. And when I'm in the water, I'm present. You forget everything, which is rare today,' he says.

Douglas points out another positive aspect:

'No one judges you on how long you are in the water, simply participating is good, and there are the dippers versus the swimmers.

'And it's so minimalist – you're getting into the water with your swimsuit and that's it,' he says.

Sauna guidelines

- *Shower before and after having a sauna.*
- *There are no rules about how long to sit in the sauna; it's completely up to you.*
- *Even a few minutes in the hot steam will bring on the magic.*
- *The main goal is to relax both body and mind.*
- *Remember to stay hydrated by drinking wate*
- *As for the löyly, the water ladled onto the sauna stove's hot rocks, courtesy holds that you ask the other sauna-goers if it's alright before pouring it on.*
- *For those who combine sauna with a cold dip in a lake or sea, there are two schools of thought. The first says go to the water first, and then warm up in the sauna, the idea being that if you get all warm, cosy and comfortable it will be much harder to go out into the cold water. The other holds that it's fine to warm up in the sauna first before heading for the water. It's up to you.*

- If there's no sauna available where you live, a steam room may provide some of the same benefits, though it may be more humid than the drier heat of a sauna.
- If you're uncomfortable going into the sauna naked, you can wrap up in a towel. Or, you could practise some sauna sisu and self-acceptance by challenging yourself to get comfortable with your own body and go in naked.

CHAPTER 5

Nature therapy: the benefits of a walk in the woods

At the top of Finland lies a region of virtually untouched wilderness, save for a few ski resorts. Called Lapland, the area stretches above the Arctic Circle across northern Finland, Sweden, Norway and into northern Russia's Kola Peninsula.

Finnish Lapland, often dubbed as one of Europe's last great wildernesses, covers about a third of Finland's land mass, measuring around 100,000 square kilometres of subarctic wilderness. With some of the purest, cleanest air on the planet along with awe-inspiring pockets of nature,

Lapland is home to the indigenous Sámi people, who number fewer than 10,000. All told, less than 4 per cent of Finland's population of 5.5 million people live in the sparsely populated region.

For many, Lapland conjures up images of Santa Claus – Finland having laid claim to being the 'official' home of Father Christmas – with pure white snow, skiing and husky rides, cosy log cabins, roaring fires and roaming reindeer.

My first trip to Finland's far north feels scripted, for it manages to squeeze in just about every element of the winter wonderland experience that people travel from all around the world to see.

It's November in the mid-2000s and I'm part of a press group that has been flown in from Helsinki, an hour's flight away, to mark the start of the ski season at a popular northern resort, Ruka. Geography sticklers may note that Ruka in Kuusamo is located just below the Arctic Circle; though it's not officially part of Lapland, most people consider it to be.

The launch party is celebrated with all manner of activities from skiing to husky rides, reindeer sightings, local cuisine and endless rounds of drinks. Indeed, the weekend pretty much sets the pattern for the many ski season openings from Levi to Saariselkä and Pyhä-Luosto that I attend during my early years working for a large magazine publisher.

As often happened during my first years in Finland, I'm totally ill equipped for spending great lengths of time outdoors doing outdoorsy things – the cliché of an urbanite who owns absolutely nothing appropriate for spending more than ten minutes outdoors, despite having braved many cold and snowy Toronto winters. Luckily, I'm able to borrow a ski jacket and trousers from a friend.

But it is not the free access to the resort's downhill ski slopes, the endless rounds of drinks or the domestic celebrities who have been flown in that leave a lasting impression on me.

For me, the indelible marks come from the authentic experiences I have there; they start me back on a path towards the natural world.

On the first evening, we are introduced to the laid-back Arctic way of life that includes an evening stroll through a moonlit forest. Snow sparkles on the branches of the great pine and spruce trees as we make our way to a picture-perfect red wooden cottage that houses a restaurant.

After our group shuffles in, we stomp the snow off our boots and remove our heavy coats. I take in the candle-lit rustic dining room where we are seated at long wooden tables and treated to an array of Lapland cuisine – unpretentious and hearty food that provides the perfect sustenance after the fresh outdoor air.

Following a meal of creamy salmon soup accompanied by rye bread and *rieska*, the potato flat bread of the region, and a dessert of *leipäjuusto* (cow's milk cheese) served with a dollop of cloudberry jam, we step back out into the clear, starry night. We file back in satisfied silence – the only sound is of the snow squeaking underfoot – along the path to the roadside clearing where our bus is parked.

Just as we reach the clearing there is a low crackling noise unlike any sound I've ever heard before. Then, on the horizon and across the sky, shades of orange, red, yellow, green and blue appear like mysterious figures dancing, swaying back and forth.

I stand there mesmerised and totally absorbed in the moment. It's seems unbelievable that nature can create such a spectacular show. Even though it lasts only a few minutes, it's more magnificent than just about anything that I've ever seen on TV or in a movie.

This is, of course, the Northern Lights, or Aurora Borealis, nature's light spectacle that is on every serious traveller's bucket list.

I realise I'm very fortunate. For while there's a good chance of seeing the Northern Lights in many northern parts of the world, especially during crisp, clear winter nights, the phenomenon is up to nature and the right set of magnetic conditions.

An oft-repeated story from Finnish mythology holds that the Northern Lights, *revontulet* or 'fox fires' in Finnish, are created when an Arctic fox runs past the mountains and grazes them with its fur, which causes sparks to fly into the sky.

Seeing the Northern Lights ignites in me an increased awareness, appreciation and gratitude for the natural world.

But I only come to understand and appreciate how rare Lapland's pristine nature is following several trips over the years to large metropolises such as Beijing, Shanghai and Bangkok. Spending time on assignments in those bustling megacities opens my eyes (and nose and throat) to how scarce clean air, pure nature and silence are in an overcrowded, noisy world.

According to the WHO, Finland's air quality was ranked as the third best in the world in 2016. In the same year, the

Katja Pantzar

Finnish Meteorological Institute recorded the cleanest air on earth in Lapland's Pallas-Yllästunturi National Park.

Nature *sisu*

Many years later, in early August, I'm on a magazine assignment at an outdoor activity summer camp at the Kiilopää Fell Centre, run by the Finnish Outdoor Association.

Nestled in Lapland's nature, the Fell Centre lies about 120 kilometres from Sodankylä, which has brought famous directors to the far north for its well-known no-VIP formalities Midnight Sun Film Festival. Everyone sits together, directors and festival-goers alike, while films are screened around the clock, as during the summer months the sun doesn't set.

The sun also shines during our camp, which is hosted by the centre's director, Seppo Uski, a cheerful man who has built a career in Lapland's hospitality industry. He starts each morning by breezing into the breakfast canteen with, 'Good Morning, there's a great day on the way!' which is perhaps not the most typical Finnish greeting.

On the second evening, I set out with the other

participants – there's around fifty of us, from infants to octogenarians – to hike up to Kiilopää's peak. It's not a strenuous walk, as the two-kilometre route runs along a well-maintained trail comprised of duckboards in several sections.

When we reach the sun-drenched 546-metre peak in the evening just after 9 p.m., I explore the rocky outcrop with the others and take in the unhindered views that stretch out in every direction.

As I stand there on the peak – cliché alert – I feel as though I'm literally on the top of the world, suspended in the moment without a care.

This type of heightened experience in nature is something I have read about, but never quite fully understood until that moment. My thoughts are not highly original, but run along the lines of: 'This is it. This is everything. Nothing else matters. I don't need anything else right now!'

I feel as though I'm literally on the top of the world, suspended in the moment without a care.

I come to view this type of authentic experience as nature *sisu* – I'm nourishing myself physically and mentally and finding a sense of peace that helps me to maintain my overall wellbeing and strengthen my *sisu*. And although our journey to the peak wasn't taxing, I still made the effort to join the evening excursion rather than choosing to laze about and watch TV in the cabin. We are a group of fellow human beings who have walked up a hill together to encounter an awe-inspiring natural view. It doesn't matter what anyone does for a living, what size their house or apartment is, or what their net worth is.

It is our host, Seppo Uski, who says: 'When you reach the top of the Kiilopää fell and you hear nothing but silence, you know you've arrived.'

Over the time at the camp, Uski often says something simple but profound. I start jotting down these 'Uskisms' in the notebook that I always carry with me.

For what he says is true. Although we are all fully clothed, wearing long sleeves and trousers to keep away the mosquitos, this experience reminds me of sitting in a sauna, where everything feels stripped away and none of the external things matter. That is a great part of the camp's brilliance.

I also notice how the silence up there on the peak makes me feel peaceful inside. It sets me thinking about how I could actively seek out more pockets of natural calm in my daily life.

We walk back down to the Fell Centre in time for an evening sauna. Perched almost atop a burbling brook and tucked away behind a row of log cabins is the cheekily named 'Cold Spa'. Two wooden cottages, one housing changing rooms and the other an authentic Finnish smoke sauna, overlook a freshwater brook that even during the summer months can be an invigorating 11 degrees Celsius or so.

A few cold-water dips in the fading evening light followed by sitting in quiet contemplation in the relaxing steam of the smoke sauna rivals just about every fancy five-star spa I've been to.

I recall Uski's introduction to the 'Cold Spa': 'You go into the water and come out a better person,' he said, echoing what so many people have told me about this transformative practice.

My nature-induced tranquillity continues the next morning as we set out on a hike along the trails that snake through the sweet-smelling pine and mountain birch forests, past the soft moss-covered forest beds.

Given Uski's apt depiction of how it felt to arrive at the peak and take a cold dip, I later ask him why he thinks the forest is so restorative. Again he delivers: 'When you stand in the forest and look up at the trees, your own problems seem small.'

I'm impressed by another excursion, a Moomin-themed walk along the forest trails. Aimed at the weekend's younger participants, this one incorporates elements of Tove Jansson's fairy tales.

Here at Kiilopää, young children between the ages of four and six head into the woods to learn about flora and fauna. They stand in silence calmly watching a reindeer that stops to graze on lichens and leaves.

Our guide, Sanna Jahkola, a young woman from Helsinki studying to be a teacher, holds the children's attention with stories and activities.

Accompanied by their parents, the children mostly listen for the duration of the three-hour walk. I watch in amazement as the youngest, then fourteen-month-old Mimosa, plops herself down by a crowberry bush and starts snacking on the berries. Her mother is Jahkola, who later tells me that her enthusiasm for the outdoors originated from her childhood, with summers spent at the family cottage in the countryside, and from an active involvement in the Scouts and Guides.

Jahkola, the mother of three children, says nature is a good learning environment, not just about the natural world but also for honing practical outdoor and safety skills.

'It also teaches social skills such as consideration for others. When you're walking through the woods and there's a branch in the way, you learn to hold it back for the next walker so they don't get hit,' she says.

Forest therapy

Green Care, forest therapy or nature therapy refers to the power of nature to provide an antidote to the stresses of modern life, boost general wellbeing and offer a much-needed digital detox. The topic has been widely studied around the world from Japan to the US, Canada, the UK and Finland.

My interest in the topic grows as I notice how much better I feel when I choose to pedal along a forested park trail instead of alongside a busy road heavy with traffic.

As I've noticed, many generations of Finns have a very close relationship with the natural world.

That observation is backed up by statistics: 96 per cent of Finns participate in outdoor recreation, on average two to three times a week, according to the Natural Resources Institute Finland (Luke). Those outdoor activities include walking, swimming in natural waters, spending time at a summer cottage, picking berries and mushrooms, bicycling, studying nature, boating, cross-country skiing, sunbathing on the beach, picnicking and collecting wood for household use.

In order to learn more about Green Care, I contact Liisa Tyrväinen, a research professor with Luke, who has devoted her career to studying the links between wellbeing, nature and outdoor recreation.

Green Care, forest therapy or nature therapy refers to the power of nature to provide an antidote to the stresses of modern life.

Tyrväinen is frequently quoted on the topic and is one of the interviewees in American journalist and author Florence Williams' book *The Nature Fix: Why Nature Makes Us Happier, Healthier and More Creative*, which delves into the science behind nature's positive effects on the brain.

Just a fifteen-minute walk in the woods can help lower stress, blood pressure and relax tense muscles, according to Tyrväinen. Her message of moderation appeals to me – you don't need to hire a Forest Therapy guide, go trail running, or go for an all-day hike to reap the benefits of Mother Nature.

I meet Tyrväinen, an energetic woman in her early fifties, on a spring day at the Viikki Nature Reserve on the outskirts of Helsinki. Located here are university research centres for agriculture and forestry and a bird sanctuary, alongside forests, fields (complete with grazing cows) and marshes.

In the spirit of Forest Therapy, we carry out our conversation while walking through the reserve's public forest paths.

I pose the question to Tyrväinen: how can spending time in a forest improve wellbeing and strengthen *sisu*?

'We can now say for certain that nature can help in the prevention of some diseases, avoid burnout, and treat symptoms of mild depression and fatigue or burnout,' she replies. 'People relax in the woods, making it an effective way to take a break from the chronic stress that's associated with many lifestyle illnesses that are prevalent today, such as type 2 diabetes.'

We stop for a moment and listen to the wood warblers singing and admire the small white wood anemones that are blooming.

In order to understand the metrics used to measure wellbeing, it's necessary to go back almost two decades.

Tyrväinen tells me that in the early 2000s, the first significant Finnish research projects on the health–nature connection were carried out. At the University of Helsinki, Tyrväinen carried out a study with researcher and psychology professor Kalevi Korpela, who is also well known for his work on wellbeing and the environment, to see whether being active in nature affected the mental health and mood of urbanites.

Later, the Finns teamed up with Japanese researchers and the Finnish Forest Research Institute, who in turn provided a mandate for a more extensive research programme into wellbeing and forests. The Japanese have been researching the physiological benefits of 'forest bathing', *shinrin-yoku*, since the 1980s.

I ask her how the benefits of a walk in the woods are gauged.

'We carry out a controlled test in a place like Helsinki Central Park. That means that when the subject arrives from work to the test he or she has eaten the same food before the visit, had the same drive time and so on. Then we sit for fifteen minutes and walk for thirty minutes. We take a range of samples, such as saliva, at various intervals to measure the change of stress hormones. Blood tests can be used to measure changes, as has been done by our Japanese colleagues. We also monitor mood changes, have heart-rate monitors to measure heart-rate fluctuation, and check blood pressure according to a specific protocol,' she explains.

Heart rate, she tells me, is one of the clearest indicators of health in this type of field experiment.

And blood pressure can be affected by air pollution, too. As is well known, high blood pressure places a strain on the heart and blood vessels, which can increase the risk of a heart attack or stroke if it continues over a longer period of time.

'If you're in a small park, you don't necessarily get clean air, which is why I've tried to emphasise the importance of large, quiet, calm areas of nature with clean air,' she says.

Noise pollution is another concern.

'As noise affects the subconscious and can be an irritant, it's an environmental disturbance that causes stress. In many cities, especially big ones, noise affects the nervous system. Noise and air pollution are among the biggest health risks in Europe and in North America, and if we think of China, it's a massive problem,' says Tyrväinen.

More than half of the world's population lives in cities. The WHO has listed seven categories of adverse health effects from noise pollution ranging from sleep and cardiovascular disturbances to hearing impairment.

Katja Pantzar

I recall reading an article many years ago in the main Finnish daily *Helsingin Sanomat* about a tourism research project in Finland's Northern Karelia into wellbeing that included a silence component. One of the interviewees, a Hong Kong native, told the paper that the first time she ever heard the sound of raindrops was in the Karelian wilds.

Tyrväinen initially studied forestry with the goal of being a forester.

'It was a male-dominated field and as a woman I wanted to have an impact – I'm all for gender equality,' she says.

But she quickly grew critical of the university teaching at the time, which was very focused on the wood production industry.

'For me, the other values of the forest for recreational purposes came up very strongly. Back then no one spoke about the health aspects, which is what I became interested in. So I set about carving my own path,' she says.

Tyrväinen grew up in the Finnish Lake District, playing on the waterfront and in the forests, picking berries and mushrooms. She echoes what so many people who value nature seem to share – a childhood in the woods sets them up for a close lifetime relationship with nature.

One of the main sources of inspiration for Tyrväinen's work has been the Finnish public.

'In our research, stories and anecdotes from ordinary people have stressed how important the forest is for them as a source of mental and physical wellbeing. People have sent me letters with accounts of how the woodlands have helped them to recover from depression, for example,' she says. 'For Finns, the forest is akin to a church or temple.'

One of the areas Tyrväinen and her colleagues are currently focusing on is expanding research into the effects of regular nature visits on lifestyle diseases such as type 2 diabetes. Could they allow patients to reduce the amount of medicine or even stop taking medicine all together?

'We're also interested in understanding the effects of urbanisation. Why are British kids scared of nature, for example? A connection to nature hasn't had the chance to evolve during childhood and parents feel their kids shouldn't go into the forest because it's not safe. It's a cultural thing. Finns still feel that the woods are a safe and natural environment for play,' she says. 'Many Finns still choose forests or nature as their favourite place. Ten years ago the figure was at 90 per cent, which is very high.'

Access to nature in Finland's cities, as in many urban areas throughout the other Nordic countries, is largely a given, although compact city policies are also much debated in Helsinki.

'One of the key tools of city planning is to ensure that we secure large green areas through urban centres.'

Tyrväinen says that one of biggest challenges is preserving this Nordic lifestyle that includes large swathes of green space that are easily accessible for urbanites.

'How do we prove those green spaces are worth saving? The challenge is producing the evidence that convinces decision-makers that nature areas need to be allocated and people need to be encouraged and supported to use them. In the long run, it's key for our wellbeing at work and in everyday life, and we see the financial savings in healthcare,' she says.

She also voices the concern that people in Finland are moving towards a virtual lifestyle that doesn't include enough nature breaks.

'With everything virtual from technology to cities, it's a way of life that seems to be taking us in a direction away from many things that are healthy,' she laments.

'People seem to go like machines. But we're not machines and then we get sick. Once you've lost your health, what do you have?

'One of the growing tourism trends is digital detox. I notice when I start to go into overdrive and read my email during my free time even though I know it doesn't improve my performance at work in the long run. Why do I do it? The senses and the brain need to rest, recover and recharge,' she says.

Digital detox doesn't have to be a retreat. Going offline in an online world can be as simple as putting your device on silent or 'busy' mode and going for a short walk in the woods or a stroll through a city park.

~~~

In Lapland I made the connection that I'd lost or perhaps never fully appreciated and understood before, despite spending time in the forests of British Columbia when I was growing up.

I'm not off hiking in the woods every weekend. But incorporating daily doses of nature into my urban life by going for a dip in the sea every morning and choosing to cycle or walk through a park or wooded area rather than along a busy city street has been a key factor in improving my wellbeing.

Those moments of silence and solitude, even if only for ten or fifteen minutes, provide me with a restorative break that helps me build up my fortitude and find balance during a busy day. They are part of my *sisu* management; shifting the focus from a busy schedule and whatever is on my mind to the calming sounds of nature lowers my stress levels and allows me to refocus before or after a long news shift, for example.

During my walking meeting with Tyrväinen she told me that a young reporter had asked her: what should you do in the woods with kids?

Moments of silence and solitude . . . provide me with a restorative break that helps build my fortitude.

She had replied: 'You don't need to do anything. When you take kids to the woods they have no problem figuring out what to do and will entertain themselves for hours. They don't need to have a built play area with equipment and instructions. The forest is a good place for developing motor skills and creativity, not to mention exposure to microbes that help them develop immunity.'

I've long observed how happy my son is playing in the forest, exploring trees, plants and insects. Simply being able to roam freely is exhilarating for a young child.

At fifteen months old, my son ran around a forested island chasing squirrels and shrieking with delight every time he saw one.

Later, when he was four, we took him to a national park on the outskirts of the city for the first time. We were concerned that he wouldn't be able to walk the entire six-kilometre route because it was too long. However, he was so excited that he practically ran it.

It was his parents who had trouble keeping up.

Green Care

- *Nature can restore us in a variety of ways, for example by helping to reduce stress and anxiety and alleviate mild depression.*
- *Even a fifteen-minute walk through a calm green area such as a park or through a forest does wonders for mind and body.*
- *Turn it into a digital detox by putting mobile devices on silent mode.*
- *Focusing on your surroundings, such as the colour of tree leaves or flowers, can be a useful technique for taking a break from whatever is on your mind.*
- *If there's no forest nearby, going for a short stroll in a city park or along a shoreline can also be very effective.*
- *Consider a nature break to be a type of sisu booster, shifting the focus from daily demands in order to restore and recharge yourself.*

CHAPTER 6

The Nordic diet: a simple and sensible approach to good health and weight loss

~~~~~

I'm standing in the checkout line at our local grocery store waiting for my turn to pay and browsing the titles on the magazine rack when I spot the cover of a well-read national weekly featuring the smiling face of a popular Finnish news anchor. The main headline, roughly translated, reads: 'If my jeans get too tight, I just go for a longer jog, but I don't compromise on food.'

That cover and its inherent philosophy echo a theme that I come across frequently in Finnish magazines and newspapers and see shared on social media. They advocate the same common-sense message: no crash diets or extreme fasts, just take a simple and sensible approach to eating. If your waistband starts to feel too tight, cut back on sweets and treats, increase your fruit and vegetable intake and ensure that you get enough physical activity.

> **'If my jeans get too tight, I just go for a longer jog, but I don't compromise on food.'**

That message seems in such sharp contrast to the clickbaity headlines that I see in the American and British magazines and newspapers that I follow online. Those headlines often run the gamut from 'Four secrets to losing weight', 'The celebrity diet that everyone's on' and 'Why sugar is the enemy' to 'Why you should never eat bananas' and 'Five foods that you should never eat'.

Trying to stay on top of it all can be overwhelming for anybody. Of course, it's a good idea to follow newsworthy science-based research on the health benefits and properties of various foods, but in an effort to be informed, it seems that eating a healthy, balanced diet has become a complicated affair for a great many people.

For years, my own diet as an adult was a far cry from my healthy upbringing by my Finnish-Canadian parents. They followed a simple and sensible Nordic approach to eating and exercise that has kept them healthy, trim and youthful to this day. They have never dieted or joined a gym.

Yet when I was young, I didn't always appreciate their approach. After all, growing up in Canada I was the immigrant kid with the funny name who was desperately trying to fit in. One of my most vivid memories is lunch-hour at elementary school, as I unsuccessfully tried to swap my Edam cheese on whole wheat for peanut butter and jam on white fluffy Wonder Bread – something that my parents *never* purchased.

Later, as an adult, I exercised my independence by eating whatever I wanted. I recklessly indulged my sweet and savoury tooth – I have both, and to this day have difficulties not eating all the biscuits or chips on the plate – and skipped meals or ate irregularly in an effort to try to keep my weight down. I didn't realise the consequences (low blood sugar, low energy, low mood) of not sticking to a regular eating pattern of breakfast, lunch and dinner.

While eating a balanced diet is important for everyone and nutritional awareness has increased in recent years, for someone who is prone to depression the benefits of paying extra attention to what they eat can be huge.

I recently came across a 2013 Finnish study, which found that a healthy diet could reduce the risk of severe depression.

In a doctoral thesis in the field of nutritional epidemiology, Anu Ruusunen carried out a study that found that junk food, sugar and processed meats were associated with elevated depressive symptoms. Ruusunen found that 'a healthy diet rich in folate, and a dietary pattern rich in vegetables, fruits, berries, wholegrains, poultry, fish and low-fat cheese, may be protective against depression'.

Across the border in Sweden, researchers at the Karolinska Institute released the results in 2017 of a study that showed that older adults who followed a healthy Nordic diet had better cognitive status than those who ate a diet that included processed and fatty foods and lots of sweets.

Now, this all sounds like common sense to me.

Simplicity on a plate

In a nutshell, the Nordic diet is a common-sense approach to eating that's rich in berries, vegetables, and oily fish. It advocates eating less red meat and more fish, snacking on berries high in antioxidants (the natural plant compounds that help to ward off cancer, heart disease and stroke, as well as other health-related illnesses) and eating rye bread, which contains at least three times more fibre than white bread and is rich in B vitamins, iron, magnesium, zinc and antioxidants. Potatoes and root vegetables are good sources of fibre, magnesium and potassium. Using oils low in saturated fats, such as canola or extra virgin olive oil, is also recommended.

My casual observation is that many people I meet in Finland and in the other Nordic countries such as Norway and Sweden share this relatively straightforward approach to eating.

It must be said that not everyone in Finland eats a healthy balanced diet, though; people do embark on fad diets, suffer from eating disorders and, as in many countries, one of the big health challenges is countering increasingly sedentary lifestyles and too much processed, sugary food.

The Finns are also not the world's slimmest people statistically speaking; they fall into the middle of recent international comparisons. But 75 to 80 per cent of Finns are doing quite all right weight wise.

Katja Pantzar

According to an extensive study 'Health Effects of Overweight and Obesity in 195 Countries over 25 Years' published in the *New England Journal of Medicine* in 2017, the US has the largest number of obese adults at almost 80 million, which is 35 per cent of the population. To provide a comparison point, 15 to 19 per cent of Finnish men and 20 to 25 per cent of Finnish women are officially obese.

According to the study's metrics, being obese means having a body mass index over 30, which in turn is considered 'a risk factor for an expanding set of chronic diseases including cardiovascular disease, diabetes mellitus, chronic kidney disease, many cancers and an array of musculoskeletal disorders'.

The culprits? Urbanisation, lack of physical activity and poor diet.

A great many of my Nordic friends and acquaintances seem to have a less complicated relationship with food compared to in the UK and North America, where food and diet are often thorny issues, with frequently changing diets and a constant look out for the new food 'enemy'.

For example, one common misconception that seems to circulate and resurface is that bananas are bad and fattening and should be avoided at all costs. Now, as bananas contain potassium, fibre and several nutrients including vitamin B6, and vitamin C (and as a bonus they come in their own biodegradable wrapping), it's not hard to argue that they make a good natural snack and a much better option than something artificial.

But I'm not a nutritional expert, as proven by my previous dietary disclosures, so I contact one of Finland's leading nutritionists Patrik Borg, who is the author of several books about eating well, to find out more about the Nordic diet and what healthy eating entails. He is also a wellness and weight-management concept creator, lecturer and blogger.

I've been following Borg's career for many years because one of his main messages appeals to me in its simplicity and ease: 'Eat well and lose weight', which is also the title (roughly translated) of one of his best-selling books in Finland.

Essentially, his message is this simple:

'Eat a balanced diet with lots of vegetables and fruit and poultry and fish and wholegrains and occasionally you can eat the burger and fries or piece of cake. You need to enjoy your food, otherwise you'll feel miserable and it will be harder to stick to eating a healthy and balanced diet.'

As someone who craves the occasional treat, this greatly appeals to me.

Katja Pantzar

Losing weight by eating well

I meet Borg, an animated forty-something with a boyish grin, in a light-filled Helsinki café housed in a building created by one of Finland's most famous twentieth-century designers and architects Alvar Aalto.

(Meeting a nutrition expert for coffee is fitting, given that Finns drink more coffee per capita than any other nation in the world – twelve kilograms per person per year, according to the International Coffee Organisation.)

I ask him to elaborate on his food philosophy of losing weight by eating well.

'By eating regular well-balanced healthy meals and good-quality food that includes plenty of vegetables, cravings for less healthy food decreases as does weight gain. A balanced diet won't be affected if you indulge in the occasional treat because you've already given yourself permission to have them, whereas if you're on a strict diet you'll be more likely to indulge in treats because they're forbidden,' he says.

I also like his positive message of moderation: 'Relaxed eating means increasing the good rather than focusing on decreasing the bad.'

So how does his food philosophy translate on a practical level?

First, Borg advocates two habits that I have noticed a great many Finns cultivate, which are eating a proper breakfast and a proper lunch.

'Is your breakfast big enough? You need energy to fuel you through the day. In Finland, a wholesome breakfast is understood and valued, so people see the wisdom of this advice. A proper lunch is a good idea as well,' he says.

Borg stresses that eating well during the day has longer-term effects, such as better sleep. If you're tired, stressed and hungry, he says, you're more likely to overeat in the evening and make unhealthy food choices, and this can negatively impact on the quality of sleep.

'Relaxed eating means increasing the good rather than focusing on decreasing the bad.'

As he speaks, I recall that one of the first things I noticed about eating habits in the Nordics was the healthy relationship to a hearty breakfast that many of my friends and colleagues seemed to share. On a press trip with a group of Nordic journalists, I noticed how my colleague and friend Senja, who I travelled with for work during the early years, would always top her morning muesli or porridge with berries and nuts, and seek out all of the fruits and vegetables from the hotel breakfast buffet regardless of where we were.

As we discuss eating habits around the world, Borg tells me that one aspect that makes his work easy is that in Finland people are well aware of the food triangle, or the plate model, which is taught from daycare onwards. 'It's such a familiar concept that it's easy to get people who are re-evaluating their eating habits on board with the ½, ¼, ¼ principle,' he says.

The Finnish plate model advocates dividing your plate into ½ vegetables – salad or fresh, grated or steamed vegetables – ¼ potatoes, rice, pasta or cereal – and ¼ protein, such as fish, poultry, meat, legumes or nuts and seeds.

Which seems so simple and easy to follow.

In typical self-critical Finnish fashion, Borg is quick to point out what could be improved: regular healthy snacks between meals.

Two strengths of the traditional Finnish diet that he highlights are rye bread and berries, which also happen to be superfoods.

Rye bread is a national favourite; the rye grain was cultivated in Finland about 2,000 years ago. Its high fibre content aids digestion and is said to have benefits such as keeping blood sugar levels steady, which offers protection from diabetes.

As for Finnish forest berries, according to the Natural Resources Institute Finland (Luke), they contain important vitamins and minerals, and are full of fibre but aren't high in calories. Berries are also rich in polyphenols, which are powerful antioxidants.

Luke lists the benefits of antioxidants: 'Antioxidants . . . may prevent cholesterol from oxidising and become the type that will line the insides of our veins. They are also thought to slow down the growth of cancer cells, reduce the formation of tumours, and control inflammatory and allergic reactions and the growth of bacteria and viruses.'

Another key element in a healthy diet is water. As Finland has one of the cleanest water supplies in the world, the tap water is pure and delicious and there's no need to buy bottled water. According to a 2017 article in the main Finnish daily newspaper, *Helsingin Sanomat*, tap water is still the country's top thirst-quenching beverage of choice.

Borg also runs a healthy-eating and weight-management consultancy, where he sees clients who feel that their eating has got out of whack and needs to be brought back on track.

He stresses the importance of understanding *why* a person's eating has gone off the rails. One of the most common reasons, he says, is emotional eating. We need to understand why someone might be replacing regular, well-balanced meals with eating a packet of biscuits or a large chocolate bar. Is to combat tiredness, for extra energy or perhaps for consolation? He says that if one of your parents rewarded you with sweets when you were younger, you may unconsciously be doing the same thing to yourself as an adult.

Though my parents did not reward me with treats as a child, as an adult I have often eaten chocolate and sweets in an effort to try to boost my energy levels, especially in the evenings. I do that much less now I've realised that I can find extra energy by heading outdoors and being active.

'It's important to acknowledge the sources of emotional eating,' says Borg. 'Everything is interconnected – if you don't sleep well and you're tired during the day you may be more likely to overeat in an attempt to gain extra energy.'

When it comes to eating, it's also important to be aware of your relationship with drinking. Borg points out: 'If you're drinking alcohol daily or in really big quantities, it's a good idea to examine the underlining reasons – is it stress or another reason?'

I ask Borg if he thinks Finns have that special fortitude when it comes to managing their health and wellbeing.

'Yes, definitely. People want to be in good shape and they go about it with *sisu* and a sensible approach. The downside of *sisu* is trying to manage everything on one's own and not asking for help.'

I'm curious to know more about Borg's own lifestyle habits and what he eats on an average day.

He says he typically starts the morning with a proper breakfast of natural yogurt with nut muesli, fruits and berries. Then, for lunch, he'll sit down for a warm meal that includes vegetables, salad and a source of protein. And for dinner he sits down with his family – he has two children – for another proper meal with the same plate model as his lunch.

And he does enjoy sweets and treats such as the traditional Finnish cardamom-flavoured *pulla* sweetbread on occasion – with a good conscience.

Borg says he doesn't watch TV, and in addition to being a very active outdoor enthusiast, he plays competitive football and squash and he also jogs.

A close relationship to nature seems to be part of the healthy eating equation for so many Finns I meet. Borg is a volunteer National Parks sponsor, which means he's tasked with protecting them and encouraging people to get acquainted with the country's many national parks. He says that it's a natural role for him, as the forest is one of his favourite places.

'Finns thrive in the woods – they spend time together and calm down. One of my favourite activities is picking mushrooms such as morels. Foraging is like a game and you gather your food at the same time, and then get to enjoy eating homemade dishes such as a mushroom risotto or pasta,' he says.

According to Luke, forest mushrooms are a good source of protein and fibre, and they also contain a range of vitamins including a number of B vitamins such as niacin, riboflavin, folate, pyridoxine and cobalamin. Mushrooms also boast immune-boosting properties and are packed with vitamin D.

Owing to Everyman's Right (*jokamiehen oikeus* in Finnish), not only is there freedom to access public or private lands for recreation; picking berries, herbs, nuts and mushrooms is also allowed.

As there are stretches of forest throughout the city centre, urban foraging in central Helsinki is an option. That means that if you know your berries and mushrooms, you can collect your supper on the way home.

The foraging season usually runs from late July to early October. It should be noted that it's important to know what you're picking, as some mushrooms, for example, are poisonous.

Picking berries and mushrooms is also a good example of Nordic practicality. Long before local food became a trend, it has been a way of life in Finland. It also strikes me as a *sisu*'ish activity – heading out to forage instead of driving to the grocery store to buy berries and mushrooms.

The edible garden

In addition to foraging rights, allotment gardens are peppered throughout the country. Like the community gardens found around the world, these plots offer the option to grow fruits, vegetables and flowers to those who don't have access to a cottage or a house with a yard.

In the Nordic countries, the first allotment garden reportedly dates back to 1655 in Denmark. From there the idea spread to Sweden, Norway and Finland.

The first Finnish allotment gardens date back to the early 1900s. Some are ownership-based and, in addition to a small plot of land, they often include a very basic cottage that's suitable for an overnight stay. Many allotment gardens are in and around cities, which makes them easily accessible by car, bicycle or public transport.

These days, growing your own food has little to do with necessity, as grocery store shelves are well stocked with a range of foodstuffs from around the world. Yet the Finnish tradition of collecting vitamin-rich berries and root vegetables during the summer months and freezing or canning them for the winter continues. This is also another excellent example of DIY *sisu*. Instead of taking the easy route of buying berries in the grocery store or ordering them online, people head out into the woods, or the garden, to forage and spend some time in nature. Foraging and gardening are activities that people – regardless of income, status or age – take great pleasure in. During the growing season, my social media feeds fill up with images of everything from colourful ripe wild berries such as raspberries, strawberries, bilberries and lingonberries – there are just under forty varieties of edible berry in Finland – to the yellow chanterelle mushrooms that are a national favourite.

While I make no claim to being a forager, my son and I do make a mean smoothie from the aronia berries plucked from the bushes by the shore in our neighbourhood. These dark purple berries contain antioxidants and are packed with vitamins such as C and E, as well as the minerals magnesium, iron and potassium.

I'm continually inspired and impressed by the practical foraging and gardening skills of so many people in Finland. My good friend Tiina makes an excellent role model for this grow-and-pick-your-own philosophy. Whenever I'm treated to a meal created by Tiina, the majority of dishes on the table are made from local ingredients that she has gathered or grown.

Like Borg's, Tiina's approach to food emphasises seasonal berries and vegetables and grains and doesn't shy away from the occasional treat such as cake or pie.

In fact, I find her approach to food downright refreshing.

'I've never been on a diet or tried to lose weight,' says Tiina, who is a size 36. 'My weight has increased slightly with age, but I believe that's natural. Personally, I think dieting is silly and can even be dangerous for some people. And often it's to no end as people gain back the weight they initially lost,' she says.

'Food is very dear to me and I'm proud that I've passed that love on to my children. Food is also a political and social issue. I want to ensure that our family doesn't eat unethically, even though social issues surrounding food are complicated. I want to ensure it is not shipped in from the other side of the world and that we don't eat too many ready-made or processed products. At the same time, ready-made foods are not always a bad thing; on the contrary, falafels and other dishes that you can buy from the supermarket are good and well made. It's all about balance,' she says.

'I don't believe in any absolutes – I like sweet things and don't think that sugar is evil. Yes, if you eat too much of it, that's not good. Some store- bought treats contain bad fats, which is why I try to bake my own desserts so that I know exactly how much sugar and fat they contain,' says Tiina.

I've never run into Tiina at our local grocery store and now I find out why: she prefers to gather her ingredients from the garden at her summer cottage and in the nearby forest.

When we speak, it's August and she says, 'Today it will probably be chanterelle mushrooms, chives and herbs on a bed of salad. Perhaps zucchini, if it's ripe.'

'I'm in tune and interested in seasonality – mushrooms, berries, edible natural plants such as nettle, dandelions and birch leaves. Each year I learn more and more about them. This summer I served my family spruce pizza, which my daughter and her boyfriend said was definitely a Finnish specialty. But they both thought it was really good,' she says.

She is also passionate about fruits and berries and tells me that she picks blueberries and lingonberries from the forest. In her summer cottage garden and small orchard she has blackberries, sour cherries, raspberries, apples and little plums. Like many Finns, Tiina makes sauces, jams and purées out of them and freezes them so they can be enjoyed throughout the year.

She also grows a range of vegetables, spices and herbs ranging from oregano, rosemary and chives, to basil and coriander.

'I love Swiss chard, and I plant different types of salads each year, and zucchini and potatoes. I also love mangold and it grows well. I plant Jerusalem artichokes, kohlrabi, wax beans, yellow beans, black beans, tomatoes and red peppers,' she says.

And she carries a Nordic Zen type of approach to nature's bounty.

'In Finland, and probably elsewhere in the world, people have a saying about what the forest or nature doesn't offer this year. I've adopted an attitude that if one specific type of berry or mushroom is not on offer, then there's something else. If the start of the season is poor for mushrooms, then perhaps the end of the season is better,' she says. 'In this day and age, a person certainly won't suffer if something isn't available.'

Cottage life

For a great many Finns, a fruit and vegetable garden are a key part of the cottage experience. Known as *mökki* in Finnish, the summer cottage is a national institution where people go to relax, rest and recharge in the countryside, preferably on the waterfront.

Though there are more than half a million cottages or leisure homes in Finland, one estimate places the number of active cottage users at three million, which is more per capita than anywhere else in the world.

Just about everyone I meet seems to go to a cottage for a week or more in the summer, whether it's their own, or one that they have access to through family or friends, or simply by renting. The key is to simply unwind and spend time in nature.

It's the quintessential break from working life – many people in Finland enjoy generous annual holidays of up to five weeks, which depends, of course, on the nature of their work.

Some cottages have all the mod cons and are winterised but many proudly celebrate getting away from it all with few frills – no electricity or running water, for example – as a way of really getting back to nature and keeping it simple.

One of the most restorative *mökki* weekends I have enjoyed was at a friend's cottage on Lake Näsijärvi near the city of Tampere. Built in the 1920s, the wooden house had a lake-top sauna, perfect for jumping into the water after a good steam, and neither electricity nor running water.

The rediscovery of simple tasks such as washing dishes by hand after a shared meal reminded me of the joys of camping as a child. There's an awareness of nature's rhythms – light and darkness set the tone for what activities could be done when and brought about a relaxed pace to each day.

One of the best-known descriptions of Finnish cottage life is from Moomin creator Tove Jansson's *The Summer Book*. In a series of timeless vignettes, Jansson eloquently captures the essence of a summer spent in a cottage on a small island in the Gulf of Finland by a grandmother and six-year-old Sophia, who is modelled on Jansson's own granddaughter. As the duo walks through the 'magic forest' and along the island's shoreline, they discuss what matters: love, life, friendship and death.

Jansson lived on an island in the Pellinge Peninsula much like the one described in her book. Her writing captures the intensity of summer, which in this part of the world is a brief affair. And therein lies part of its captivating spell.

Living in a northerly location with four distinct seasons that include long winters and short summers has taught me gratitude for each season and to pay attention to details such as the ever-changing Nordic light. As light is a seemingly endless resource during the summer months and a precious fleeting commodity during the dark winter months, it has become a quality that I pay attention to in a way I never did before.

~

Tiina has a lovely wooden cottage painted red with a blue front door that's about a forty-five-minute drive from Helsinki into the countryside. The modest two-storey wooden cottage was built in the late 1800s and then expanded in the 1940s when it operated as the village shop for several years. When Tiina and her family acquired it almost twenty years ago, it belonged to a notable ceramicist and artist.

Naturally I ask Tiina what the cottage means to her. I find her answers to so many of my questions thoughtful, wise and worthy of translation.

'It's a place for relaxation and variation and is visually always wonderful as the scenery changes with each season. It's a place for the family on weekends and holidays. My adult children and their spouses have their own rooms, so we can all be together, but with our own space,' she says.

'The cottage is important for me because it's close to the forest and the yard. I can go swimming, summer and winter, as there's an *avanto* (a winter swimming spot) maintained by the municipality. In the winter, I cross-country ski if there's snow. With my family we explore the nature trails in the woods. In the autumn I spend a lot of time in the forest, perhaps too much. It's like an addiction. I try to think of it as incidental exercise.'

Nordic diet tips

- *Keep it simple: think of the plate model and aim for a meal that's ½ vegetables – salad or steamed vegetables – ¼ potato, rice, pasta or cereal, and ¼ protein, such as fish, poultry, meat, legumes, nuts and seeds.*
- *When selecting food at the grocery store look at your basket or cart. Does it reflect the plate model with a lot of vegetables and fruits? One commonly used aid is to think of a rainbow: does your selection of vegetables and fruits have a wide variety of colours?*
- *Add fruits and berries to your morning porridge or cereal, or eat them as a healthy snack.*
- *Eat with the seasons.*
- *Prefer water as a thirst-quenching drink of choice.*
- *If picking your own produce is not possible, consider growing tomatoes or herbs in window boxes.*
- *Farmers' markets or pick-your-own farms offer another option that's especially popular with kids.*
- *Foraging tours provide a great way of learning about wild eats available close to where you live.*

CHAPTER 7

Getting a healthy start: cultivating *sisu* from early childhood

~~~~~

I meet my future husband on a train from Helsinki to St Petersburg. We're both part of a press trip; I'm there as a journalist and he's been invited along as the good friend of one of the trip's organisers, filling in for a last-minute cancellation.

Born in India but raised in Finland from the age of five, Tino is handsome, charismatic and cosmopolitan. He speaks several languages and unbeknownst to me at the time he is a domestic celebrity, having performed in successful theatre productions and hosting a popular TV show in the late 1990s.

As we talk, I have this strange feeling of familiarity, as though we already know each other. He reminds me of my Canadian friends, who I miss. In fact, my first impression is that he must have lived in North America, because he speaks near perfect English and is friendly and good at small talk in a charming American sort of way. But although he's travelled very widely, it turns out that he's never been to Canada.

He is the life of the party and we spend a lot of time together over the course of the weekend. After the trip, we hang out back in Helsinki and get to know each other before our friendship develops into a romance.

And from there, things move quickly. After dating for about eight months, he proposes, I accept and we marry. And little over a year later, in early 2010, our lovely son is born, which is how I come to experience the Finnish maternity and childcare system first-hand.

The famous baby box

There are a great many perks to being pregnant in Finland, such as regular prenatal exams, counselling on how to stay healthy during pregnancy and always getting a seat on the bus (I stop cycling for the unborn baby's safety). But by far one of the most memorable pregnancy moments is the arrival of the much-lauded baby box, which is essentially a starter-kit for parents-to-be.

The Finnish maternity-package concept has attracted substantial international interest, especially following media reports on the topic. The idea continues to spread around the world; states such as New Jersey and countries including Scotland have started offering baby boxes in recent years. A number of private companies around the world have also capitalised on the idea, selling different versions of the same concept.

On a dark December afternoon, when I am about eight months pregnant, I go to the post office to pick up the box, which contains just about everything we will need for the first few months of our baby's life – ranging from a sleeping bag to reusable cloth diapers – all contained in a sturdy box. Though much has been written about the cardboard box doubling as a crib, I don't personally know of any families in Finland who actually use it as a crib for baby to sleep in; the most common use seems to be for storage!

Back at home in the evening my husband and I unpack the box, marvelling at all the items (around fifty) that are included, with little idea yet of how useful virtually every item will be.

Among the carefully packed articles are practical necessities such as baby-proof nail scissors (who knew that a new-born's fingernails would grow so quickly and require regular trimming?), a soft hairbrush and sets of soft cotton outfits – pants and tops – in gender-neutral colours. There's a bib, a full winter suit, complete with hat, booties and mittens, a thermometer to ensure baby's bathwater is not too hot – and even a book for baby, *Iloinen lorutoukka* (that roughly translates to: 'The Happy Nursery Rhyme Caterpillar'), which seems fitting for a country ranked as one of the world's most literate nations.

There's also an emphasis on sustainability; for example, many of the clothes are made from recycled fabrics and favour eco-friendly textiles whenever possible.

It could be said that the roots of the Finnish maternity package lie in a type of *sisu* – dealing with adversity and coming up with a solution. The maternity-package concept was introduced to address a specific challenge in the late 1930s in Finland: low birth rates and high infant mortality rates. Along with ensuring access to public health services for all Finnish mothers, the box was key in helping Finland tackle the latter problem – in the late 1930s one in ten infants died during their first year of life. By 2015, Finland had one of the world's lowest infant mortality rates.

Today the maternity package is available to all expectant parents in Finland.

The early years

After our son is born, we adjust to being new parents and our new, sleep-deprived reality of being a family with an infant.

I experience a bout of post-natal depression that in hindsight was so clearly brought on by the storm of hormones, the major life change, and a lack of sleep and exercise. Until this point in my stay in Finland much of my overall wellbeing has flowed quite effortlessly, so I'm not yet aware of how vigilant I need to be about maintaining a balance that includes plenty of exercise and rest.

Add to that some doses of serious naivety on my part in thinking that having a baby would be predominantly about cute outfits, cuddles and photo ops. After all, I babysat extensively as a teenager and later as a godmother. I adore babies and children. I thought I knew what taking care of a little person entailed . . .

The reality of being responsible for a small infant 24/7 combined with the fact that I'm used to working full-time and being relatively independent, means, however, that I'm in for a big life change. Despite help from friends and family, I find it challenging spending long stretches at home alone with a baby for the duration of the very generous one-year-long maternity leave that I, like many new mothers in Finland, are allowed to take.

My feeling of isolation increases when I find myself sitting bleary-eyed at parent and baby groups in an effort to get out and be more social and ensure that my little boy gets all the things he needs. But as I didn't grow up in Finland, I don't know any of the Finnish baby songs. This only compounds the sense of inadequacy I feel when I compare myself to the supermums who have lost all their pregnancy weight – it takes me several years to do that; it's not until I discover winter swimming that I fully manage it – or whose babies sleep through the night, or who make their own organic baby food from Finnish berries (naturally) and dress their offspring in stylish outfits.

But, thankfully, we realise that I'm depressed and we seek out and quickly receive professional help, which includes talk therapy, something that I have greatly benefited from at other points during my life. This helps me realise how invaluable and beneficial it is to talk about what's bothering me and making me anxious, rather than trying to be consistently resilient – or have too much *sisu* – and deal with everything on my own.

This is a lesson that I apparently need to keep relearning. When I actually share my anxieties, fears or concerns with other people, it turns out that a great many can relate to them. People are supportive and understanding. No one seems to expect me to try to achieve the unrealistic, perfectionistic expectations I set for myself. The simple process of articulating and sharing a concern out loud, whether with a therapist or a friend, makes it less overwhelming.

Through talking with therapists, I realise what seems fairly obvious in hindsight: I was being very hard on myself because I felt that I wasn't doing a good enough job as a new mother. It turns out that this is a common situation for new mothers, especially those who have children later on in life. It took me a while to accept that despite my best intentions, some days the laundry didn't get done. And that was absolutely fine.

One morning we wake up feeling refreshed and realise that the whole family has slept through the entire night without any interruptions.

By this time, I'm back at work full-time and our son, now a toddler, is immersed in the Finnish day-care system, which is quite amazing, especially when I compare notes with my friends who have young children in other countries.

Not only is the Finnish system well organised – we have been incredibly lucky in that our day-care (and later pre-school and school) is within a five-minute walk of our home – it is a functional, sensible system run by professionally trained early-childhood carers and teachers.

There are no televisions or iPads. It's not a babysitting service: young children five years old and younger learn to socialise, play together, sing, do constructive arts and crafts, use a knife and fork and spoon, and eat relatively balanced meals all served by the day-care. We don't need to pack lunches or bring food.

As I later learn, the free meal perk continues through the school system; each child is served a hot lunch each weekday. The idea of this common good – learning doesn't happen on an empty stomach and every single child should be fed – dates back to 1943 when it was initiated during wartime. Finland was the first country to start the practice and it continues to this day. It may not be gourmet food, but it ensures that children don't go hungry.

The pre-school years

While our son is in day-care, until he starts pre-school at the age of six, the cost is a capped rate based on a percentage of our earnings. That rate then drops as he's in pre-school for half of the day, which is free. (Primary and secondary school are also free in Finland and university education is virtually free for Finnish and EU residents.)

When I listen to the stories of my friends with young children who live in countries where there is little or no public day-care, I cannot help but feel incredibly fortunate.

Like my friends in Canada and the US, several of my British friends with young pre-school-age children cobble together a patchwork schedule of a few days a week of work, with mother and father staying at home on certain days, if possible. Or they end up hiring a costly nanny or sitter, unless they're fortunate enough to have friends or family living within helping distance.

For comparison, a 2016 OECD Social Indicators report found that Canadian families spend 32.3 per cent of their income on childcare, while in the UK a two-income family paid about 33.8 per cent of their income on childcare. For Finland it was 17.1 per cent.

As a working mother, I come to view organised and subsidised child-care as an equality and wellbeing issue because it ensures that women can work and continue their careers.

It also gives me new insight and understanding as to why Finland ranks high on certain international surveys. In 2014, for the second time, Finland was voted the best country in the world to be a mum by Save the Children's Mothers' Index, a report that ranks the wellbeing of mothers and children in 178 countries based on health, nutrition, education and economic and political status.

Part of the reason the Finnish public childcare system was developed as such was so that women could participate in the workforce and contribute to the economy. But it is also about rights: one of the reasons Finland is considered to be a gender-equality pioneer is because it was one of the first countries to give women the right to vote, which it did in 1906, and to stand in elections, which it did the same year.

~~~~

Another aspect that stands out is that year-round in Finland children play outdoors. Rain, shine or snow, every day in day-care and pre-school they spend time at the local playground, the only exception being if temperatures dip below a certain point.

In the day-care and pre-school system, all the kids have proper raingear and warm winter overalls along with hats, scarves and mittens.

This seems like good *sisu* training to me, for early on children are taught a hardy approach to heading outdoors as part of a healthy daily routine. I come across this head-outside-whatever-the-weather sensibility in several other Nordic countries from Norway to Iceland. They all have a variation of the same saying based on the general idea that there's no such thing as bad weather, just inappropriate clothing.

Early on children are taught a hardy approach to heading outdoors as part of a healthy daily routine.

In several Nordic countries there's a tradition of putting babies outside in their prams to sleep, even in the depths of winter. So long as they are well bundled up, it's thought that fresh air is good for them. In Finland, many trace the practice back to legendary Finnish paediatrician Arvo Ylppö (1887–1992), who encouraged the approach in the 1920s as a way to counter poor-quality indoor air and rickets. At a time when the child mortality rate was much higher than it is today, it was thought that fresh air and sunshine – vitamin D – would be helpful.

To this day it's not uncommon to see prams with napping infants on porches and parked outside cafés or shops during the winter months. In fact, a 2011 study by doctoral candidate Marjo Tourula found that children slept two and a half times longer when they were put outside to sleep.

This resilient *sisu* approach also trains us as parents. We quickly learn that on the weekends, there's nothing better than heading out for an hour or two to the local playground, park or forest with our son, who can run and play. And then we have a calm child, who is ready for lunch and a nap.

Our neighbourhood, like much of the rest of Helsinki and other cities in Finland, is full of public playgrounds equipped with the usual features – climbing frames, slides, swings – but also something less common: sturdy large wooden toy boxes full of toys such as spades and buckets, balls, trucks and cars. In some neighbourhoods the boxes are unlocked and in others they are locked but local residents can obtain a key; while the children are at the playground they can use and share the toys. It seems like a good practice in sharing, particularly important in an age where one of the problems plaguing the planet is too much stuff.

The school years

Finnish children start school at the age of seven whereas in the UK children start school at five, and in Canada at age five or six.

The relatively late start for Finnish school children often surprises people, especially those who follow the global educational comparisons in which Finland usually ranks near the top.

The Finnish education system has been closely followed around the world since the first PISA results in 2001 when, of all the OECD countries, Finland was the highest performer in reading literacy, mathematics and science. Though Finland has not consistently retained the number one position since then, it has remained near the top. It seems that a week doesn't go by without a positive article in the international press about the Finnish education system being shared on social media.

I have yet to experience a full year of the Finnish school system first-hand, as my son has just started first grade, but it seems that part of the key to its success – educationally and otherwise – are the nurturing day-care and pre-schools. There, kids are allowed to be kids, play together and have naps; they are not aggressively academically prepped.

Sisu for kids

Many of the skills my son learns in day-care and pre-school instil a sense of practical *sisu*, an attitude of not quitting or giving up when faced with a challenge, whether that's putting together a difficult puzzle or resolving a dispute with another child by talking it out. Early on, a sense of independence and autonomy are fostered, which can be as simple as carrying your own plate and cutlery to the dirty dish cart after you've finished eating or putting on your own snowsuit. Creative DIY skills such as making a ring as a Mother's Day gift out of a discarded button and leftover small metal hoops fosters a recycling or up-cycling way of thinking, and encourages a mindset that first explores ways to utilise used items rather than throwing them in the garbage and rushing out to buy a ready-made gift.

What I observe during the years that our son is in day-care and later pre-school is a commitment to equality, which means that every child is treated as an individual with a common-sense preventative approach in mind. This means that from an early age – three, four or five years old – children and their parents are offered any extra resources or help that they might need, ranging from speech therapy (useful for many kids, including those who are bi- or trilingual) to physical therapy.

The skills my son learns in day-care . . . instil a sense of practical *sisu*, an attitude of not quitting or giving up when faced with a challenge

As educator, author, scholar, international speaker and former director general of the Finnish Ministry of Education, Pasi Sahlberg writes in his bestselling book *Finnish Lessons 2.0:* 'Pre-school in Finland doesn't focus on preparing children for school academically. Instead, the main goal is to make sure that all children are happy and responsible individuals.'

Cultivating happy and responsible kids throughout day-care and pre-school helps to nurture *sisu*, as they then start school with a strong foundation that encourages independence and a spirit of not giving up.

Professor Sahlberg is synonymous with Finnish education on the international stage. Chances are that just about any article or report discussing education and Finland has a reference to Sahlberg and/or his extensive body of work.

On a rainy autumn Saturday afternoon slick with bright orange, yellow and red leaves dotting the sidewalks, I meet Sahlberg in the atrium of the Helsinki Music Centre. The glassy modern masterpiece houses the Sibelius Academy, the country's top music education institute, as well as the headquarters of the Finnish Radio Symphony Orchestra and the Helsinki Philharmonic Orchestra.

Against the backdrop of an open house music session, I ask Sahlberg how the early-childhood education and pre-school system contribute to the success of the Finnish education system as a whole.

'Pre-school is often defined as the year before a child goes to school, but in Finland it's broader than that – it's actually from pre-birth to the moment when a child starts school. And that's an increasingly important factor behind the successful educational performance of students later on,' says Sahlberg.

He outlines three key areas of focus: play, trust and health.

'What makes the Finnish approach unique is the emphasis on free, unstructured child-centred play. We understand that play is important for growing up, building identity and self-esteem. We also understand that children need time to do that,' says Sahlberg, whose next book will focus on the importance of play in education. 'Children will grow healthier and happier if we adults consider play an important part of the overall teaching in schools.'

'We also trust people and trust our children much more than anywhere else, we can let them play in the playground outside with other kids and just hang out,' he says. This of course is possible as Finland is a relatively safe country.

'And another key issue is health: prenatal health, the healthcare of mothers and of the infants when they are born. We have a policy that allows one of the parents to stay home with the child until they're three years old, if they choose. These are much more health-related than education-related issues, as we have this comprehensive approach in understanding the importance of childhood,' he says.

'We have all sorts of rights for children regarding their learning and wellbeing and health: for example, children have the right to fifteen minutes of each school hour for themselves during which they often go outside,' he says. That means for every forty-five minutes of school instruction children are given a fifteen-minute break.

I ask him the question that is so often posed to me by acquaintances and friends around the world: what makes the Finnish education system so good?

'Education is much more than achieving high test-scores in reading, maths and science,' he asserts.

'The strength of the Finnish system is the national approach in which we try to help everybody to be successful. We pay particular attention to those children who come from families where there's only one parent, or have parents who don't speak Finnish, or are unemployed. The whole system is designed to pay more attention and provide resources to those children,' he explains.

In international rankings, Finland scores well on equality. It has the second lowest inequality among children in the world, according to UNICEF's 'Fairness for Children: A League Table of Inequality in Child Wellbeing in Rich Countries.' And Finnish children have the third most secure childhood in the world, according to Save the Children's *Stolen Childhood: End of Childhood* report of 2017.

I ask Sahlberg if children are taught *sisu* in school in Finland.

'Finnish schools don't teach *sisu* as a topic, rather it's part of the culture in many schools. My experience is that children in Finland are taught early on that you need to finish what you start regardless of how hard the task at hand is. I believe that our schools focus on resiliency and perseverance in teaching and learning; we probably value more complex and open-ended learning experiences that often come with the sense of *sisu*. I also think that the key aspect of Finnish schools to teach children to take responsibility for their own actions and learning early on is an important factor in growing up with the *sisu* ethos,' he says. 'Some suggest that this old mentality of *sisu* would be in decline now in Finland among young people. If it is true, then perhaps teaching *sisu* more directly wouldn't be a bad idea at all.'

Another aspect that sets Finland apart is that all primary school teachers hold master's degrees.

'We've had academic, research-based education for all teachers including pre-school teachers since the late 1970s. All teachers in primary, secondary and upper secondary schools and vocational schools are doing their work with an advanced degree. No other country is doing that,' he says.

Being a teacher is a highly respected and popular profession; in some areas of the country less than 10 per cent of applicants are accepted into the five-year master's degree programme.

Teachers are given a fair amount of independence and are trusted to do their jobs in the way they see best. Standardised testing and government inspections are not part of the formula.

'A culture of trust is a hallmark of Finnish society as a whole, but particularly important in education. We have this wide and deep professionalism in our system and the luxury of having a culture within the education system that is based on trust,' says Sahlberg.

Sahlberg underlines the Finnish culture of trust – not merely in education. He says it takes the view that if you trust someone to do something, they'll do a much better job than if there's an inherent sense of distrust about whether they'll perform and there are all manner of controls and regulations.

As we chat, I ask Sahlberg whether he thinks there's an element of that special Finnish resilience *sisu* in the turning around of the Finnish school system, which half a century ago was described by many as mediocre, at best.

'Sure,' he replies. 'I would add a caveat, which is that Finns are good at creating new things and new ideas, but it mostly happens when they've got their back against the wall.'

'This education system was designed in the 1960s when the consensus in parliament at the time was that we had nothing in the country except our minds; just about everybody agreed that we had to figure out how to make the best use of our human capital. The discussion of what the school system should look like followed. Most people agreed that the system we had then was not going to do it: if we continued on that path it would segregate and divide the country, which was the last thing we needed,' explains Sahlberg.

'For me, *sisu* is in building an education system unlike in Sweden, America, England or other countries, which are addicted to reform and to continually changing things. We don't think like that. We think that you have to have an idea and then you have to implement it. This is where *sisu* comes into the picture: we don't give up, we push through. When hard times hit – and this is the beauty of Finland – when the going gets tough many other countries tighten their grip with more control. What Finns do is they let go. They understand that *sisu* doesn't come from holding on harder, *sisu* comes from allowing people to figure out what they're going to do next,' he explains.

'If there's one general thing to be underlined in the Finnish education story, it's finding a smarter way to do things. This we understand in Finland very well – not just in schools, but in working life as well, we have long holidays, people don't work at the weekends and they take a lunch-time break. Finding balance is a good thing,' he says.

It seems to me that this balance is a good way to maintain *sisu* by taking care of your overall wellbeing.

They understand that *sisu* doesn't come from holding on harder, *sisu* comes from allowing people to figure out what they're going to do next.

~~~

It would be naïve to say that everything is perfect in Finnish education. It's not. As in many countries, there are a range of issues that affect children, from concerns about potential funding cutbacks to bullying and violence. There are also worries that children spend too much time online, have declining reading skills, are not active enough and don't eat a healthy diet, which seem to parallel many of the concerns of parents and educators in other countries.

To encourage more physical activity, the Finnish government's recent education guidelines include the following recommendation: 'The day of a child aged under eight should include at least three hours of exercise. It should consist of light physical activity, brisk outdoor exercise and very energetic physical activity.'

The recommendations also highlight the importance of sufficient rest and sleep and healthy nutrition.

I meet up with Sanna Jahkola, the outdoor guide who I first met in Lapland. For in addition to studying to be a teacher, Jahkola is part of an outdoor education component to Finnish Schools on the Move, a national action programme aimed at promoting a physically active culture in comprehensive school, which is from age seven to sixteen.

I'm curious to know how the government's guidelines relate to someone who is in the field.

'The new school curriculum is terrific because different learning environments such as nature are emphasised big time – it doesn't have to be only the classroom. It can be a schoolyard, shoreline, beach or city park, not necessarily a forest,' says Jahkola, who is writing her PhD dissertation on outdoor learning.

'For children, it's a totally different learning environment, there's more room and space. We know that we feel better outdoors and children develop fine and gross motor skills as they move on uneven surfaces such as the forest floor,' says Jahkola. She adds that kids who move a lot in nature are often in better physical shape than those who don't. 'It also shows in their other activities and hobbies; for example, they choose to walk or bicycle as a form of transportation as opposed to being chauffeured around by car,' says Jahkola.

The outdoors neatly helps to cultivate three different skill sets, she says. Learning by doing, for example identifying and counting different types of trees, strengthens cognitive skills. Movement, whether walking from one place to another or keeping active to stay warm during the cold months, encourages kids to be active, and in the process of being outdoors children develop a relationship with, and a respect for, nature.

'Here we experience nature as empowering and calming, but that's not the case for everyone; in some cultures people are scared of the outdoors,' she says.

A lack of fear is something that seems to be prominent in Finland. Young children, seven or eight years old, walk, bike or take public transport to school on their own throughout the country and in the capital, which is a relatively safe city. The physical movement of young children is in sharp contrast to how my friends' children get to school in many cities in North America, which is by car, even for short distances.

I come across the Active Healthy Kids Canada 2014 Report Card on Physical Activity for Children and Youth, entitled *Is Canada in the Running?: How Canada Stacks Up Against 14 Other Countries on Physical Activity for Children and Youth*. It found that kids in Finland were raised to be active commuters. In Finland, 74 per cent of children walk or cycle to school so long as their journey is between one and three kilometres. It also found that nearly all children living 1 kilometre or less from their school commute actively.

In Canada, the same report found that 62 per cent of kids between the ages of five and seventeen were driven to school by car.

Certainly there are issues in different countries ranging from important safety concerns to long distances that necessitate a car as a means of travel. But in places where it is a viable option, encouraging kids to safely walk or cycle to school encourages their independence, a great *sisu*-building block for children.

Sisu for kids

'Unstructured outdoor play rain or shine. Weather should not be an excuse.'

Education expert Pasi Sahlberg

- *Encourage a connection with nature; it's a great place to learn about protecting the environment, animals, insects, plants, trees and flowers.*
- *Let kids climb, jump and run outdoors.*
- *Play together in a pile of autumn leaves with your kids or go for an evening stroll with flashlights.*
- *Instead of buying ready-made toys and games, let kids build things out of used cereal boxes or other items headed for the recycling bin or garbage.*
- *Play can help to develop a range of skills, from creativity to counting.*
- *Cultivate a supportive environment for not giving up if something doesn't work out immediately – some of life's greatest joys come from overcoming challenges, not from taking the easy way out.*

CHAPTER 8

Pedalling to happiness (and health)

~~~~~~

On a very chilly spring morning I'm cycling past Helsinki's north harbour, where several majestic wooden sailing ships are docked, on my way to work a news shift, when I hear a soft noise that sounds like wind chimes.

It's quite early, about 6.30 a.m. Against the backdrop of the rising sun, the sky is marbled with colour. There's not much traffic, with the exception of a few folk walking their dogs and some fellow cyclists, presumably commuting to work.

Mesmerised by the sound, I slow down to investigate. Then I realise that the melody is coming from the water, as small waves gently carry thin sheets of ice that collide with each other, creating a magical sound.

A few passers-by stop and listen for a moment, before smiling at one another and continuing on their respective journeys without saying a word.

~~~~

These types of nature moments in an urban setting have become increasingly common for me. Daily actually. For in addition to my dips in the sea, I choose cycling routes that wind along the waterfront and through the city's parks and forests whenever possible.

Not only do my cycles energise and sustain me, I learn to pay attention to what I see along the way because I'm not in a car or bus. This perspective provides a fresh focus and source of wonder – sometimes I stop to a take a photograph of the light or the leaves or the snow – while instilling a new sense of gratitude: the joy of a sunny day is much greater when it's not a daily occurrence.

I learn to pay attention to what I see.

As I'm cycling every day, I'm experiencing first-hand how nature changes with each of the four distinct seasons. I marvel at the elements as I've never done before: how the frozen ice formations on the seashore alter depending on whether the shoreline is rocky or sandy, how snow can be a wet and slushy nuisance, or a source of amazing beauty, and I wonder at the winter season's first snowflakes.

I recall Professor Hannu Rintamäki's reply when I asked him what he likes about the cold: 'Each year, winter and its pure clean ice are forever-changing elements of interest.'

In fact, one aspect I didn't initially understand during my early years here was how as soon as the sun came out, especially during the winter months, everyone headed outdoors to maximise the experience.

The dramatic Nordic light becomes a source of inspiration for me as it morphs from a precious commodity during the dark winter months into an endless source of illumination during the height of summer.

My relationship to cold weather also changes. Winter is no longer an inconvenience, which is largely how I experienced it so many years ago when I moved from the milder climate of Vancouver to the chill of Toronto, where I wore two heavy coats one on top of the other during my first winter there.

Even biking on a miserable wet dark day becomes a *sisu*-boosting exercise; yes, I can do it. I'm not going to leave my bike at home just because the weather is not optimal.

I'll approach it in the same way that a young child eagerly puts on rain boots for the joy of jumping in puddles. I know that I will feel much better, happier and more energetic if I bike – that adrenalin rush and blast of bracing air and exercise will carry me through the day. My brain also gets a boost from the movement and fresh air that is unparalleled by even the strongest cup of coffee. The elements energise me.

Cycling *sisu*

Initially, I am schooled in Nordic practicality – and *sisu* – by observing my colleagues in my first job. I notice that many of the year-round cyclists share a fortitude and positive energy.

Some commute an eighteen-kilometre round-trip a day. But relatively few seem to complain about the ride or the weather conditions. Instead, they trade stories of bravery and useful tips such as: cycling in sleet is best addressed by wearing ski glasses or goggles in order to maintain good visibility. They also often provide animated accounts of their journeys, replete with wildlife spottings if their route takes them through a forest, for example.

Many have a functional system of storing their change of clothes in panniers or a knapsack, and keeping a towel and toiletries in a locker at work so they can freshen up and change before starting the workday. Just about everyone seems to own proper weather-appropriate gear for cycling (or walking or even skiing) to work. Which is something that in my previous urban existence I didn't own. But, gradually, following their example and through sheer necessity I build up a handy kit. Biking in minus 10 degrees Celsius weather demands essentials such as a warm hat that fits under a helmet, proper gloves and footwear, and a water-resistant and well-insulated jacket and trousers.

I upgrade my vintage Jopo bike for a second-hand Aino Helkama, a sturdy black city bike modelled on a design from the 1920s. I later splurge on a new version of the same bike with seven gears, which I've had for several years now and have no plans of replacing. Not only is it handy for zipping around town during the summer, it's invaluable during the slippery winter months when parts of Helsinki are covered in sheets of ice: a slightly heavier bike equipped with studded tyres actually feels more stable than walking, as the wheel's spikes better grip the ice.

My bike also represents Nordic practicality. It is neither flashy nor has hundreds of gears. But it is reliable and well made and just right for getting from A to B. Its acquisition also represents part of my simplification process: I invest in a good-quality bike that will last so that I don't need to get a new one every few years because the old one is falling apart.

Over time I can often guess who has cycled or walked to work in an editorial office or a newsroom because they are slightly more energetic and upbeat, especially during the dark winter months that can cause seasonal affective disorder (SAD) for some, or generally make people feel a little less than lively.

Like my daily dips in the sea, this *sisu*-building activity becomes a habit. It's an investment in my wellbeing. I wake up and get my blood flowing as I cycle to work. My brain turns on and I come up with ideas. At the end of the day, I pedal away my stress.

As well as maintaining my wellbeing, I get a load of spin-off health benefits. Pedalling up hills keeps my thighs and calves in relatively good shape and gives me a bit of a cardio workout. If I don't do any other form of exercise, I'm getting some physical activity – easily up to an hour daily if I have a thirty-minute bike ride in each direction to one of my gigs.

Cycling daily also means that I can have dessert: at one point the city's online public transport planner had an option that showed you how many pieces of chocolate you could eat if you biked your route instead of taking a tram, train or bus.

There's a growing body of research on the health, and other, benefits of cycling regularly. For example, a Swedish study published in 2016 in the *Journal of the American Heart Association* found that cycling to and from work could reduce the risk of high blood pressure, obesity, high cholesterol and diabetes, and a Danish study published in 2016 found that cycling for an hour a week could reduce the risk of heart disease.

The benefits of the two-wheeler

My new Nordic definition of luxury means not having to own a car and being free of the costs associated with maintaining, fuelling, insuring and parking it. This is a relatively normal approach in the Nordics and many parts of Europe, but for someone who has grown up in a car-centric culture it represents a shift in thinking.

My new Nordic definition of luxury means not having to own a car.

I don't have anything against cars and I don't consider myself to be a bicycling activist, but it seems to me that cycling neatly addresses many issues facing the world today – from traffic congestion to pollution and health concerns arising from sedentary lifestyles.

One of the best summaries of the benefits of cycling that I have come across ran in the Copenhagen Institute for Future Studies' *Scenario* magazine some years ago. In a 2013 cover story entitled 'The Bicycle – The Future Means of Transportation', the magazine listed the many assets of the humble two-wheeler over other forms of transport:

'The bicycle is splendidly suited for a future world characterised by climate change, peak oil, obesity epidemics and a rising population pressure, particularly in cities. It is a simple means of transportation that is easy to build and repair, and it doesn't pollute or take up much space in dense city environments. In addition, the bicycle is independent of fossil and nuclear energy sources, and it provides exercise to a population that moves too little and eats too much. Finally, it is eminent for transporting small amounts of goods over short distances,' writes Danish futurist Klaus Æ. Mogensen.

In Europe, the Netherlands is known as one of the world's top cycle-savvy countries. In the Nordics, the Danish capital of Copenhagen boasts more bicycles than cars, a milestone that was reached in 2016. Indeed, the dynamic Danish political drama series *Borgen* features many of its lead characters, including politicians and journalists, whizzing around the city on their two-wheelers all year round.

In Helsinki, the city's goal is to increase the number of trips made by bicycle to 15 per cent of all trips made by 2020. The current figure stands at about 10 per cent, which is relatively good in an international context, says Niklas Aalto-Setälä, a rosy-cheeked young man in his mid-twenties and the city's cycling coordinator.

'According to Copenhagenize [an urban planning consultancy specialising in bicycle culture and traffic], we're in the top twenty cycling cities in the world,' he says.

The Finnish capital has an ambitious plan, which is to have the city centre almost – but not totally – car-free by 2025 through a mobility-on-demand initiative that would integrate all forms of shared and public transport into a single network. Facilitating cycling and walking figures strongly into this plan.

While cutting back on traffic emissions is a goal, there's also a strong health factor that comes into play.

According to the City of Helsinki, a report on the benefits and costs of cycling that was released in 2013 found that an annual investment in cycling of 20 million euros would have a cost–benefit ratio of nearly 1:8, meaning that an investment of one euro would produce benefits worth eight euros.

I ask Aalto-Setälä to expand on what those benefits are.

'Cycling has proven health benefits. When we get people to be more active and pedal instead of driving or sitting in a bus, we save a lot of healthcare costs,' explains Aalto-Setälä. 'We also know that brain activity increases whenever you exercise.'

Cycling has proven health benefits.

'Cycling reduces the risk for cardiovascular disease and depression, for example. If people visit the doctor less, it reduces overall healthcare budget costs. Also, the precise number is 7.8 – one euro of investment generates 7.8 euros in savings, which sounds high and is high regarding any infrastructure project. But if you look at the numbers for the UK, for example, they have similar cost–benefit ratio numbers that are up to 1:14,' he explains.

'When we build some new stretches of cycling paths in the city centre it saves time for many people, as it's a faster way of getting from A to B. Time costs money, of course.

There are also environmental benefits, but they're not as tangible,' he says.

'Our philosophy, which we've modelled after the Danes and the Dutch who are the best in the world when it comes to cycling, is that if a kid who's seven years old can bike by themselves from place A to place B then it's safe for everyone. Then the infrastructure is good and anyone – including eighty-year-olds – can cycle,' he says.

Icy cycles

Cycling ranks as the second-most popular form of exercise in Finland in national surveys, while walking is the first.

There's a strong winter-cycling culture in many Finnish cities and communities accompanied by a refreshing attitude that it's not a big deal to pedal in arctic conditions. In my travels, especially up north, I've seen people of all ages from young children to octogenarians confidently pedalling through snowy streets.

Granny bikes (*mummopyörä* in Finnish), a simple old-school-style women's bike with no gears that anyone can ride, are popular with riders of all ages, partly because they're surprisingly sturdy in extreme weather conditions.

On the same trip to Oulu that I meet with my cold expert professor Hannu Rintamäki, I meet Timo Perälä, a key figure in organising the world's first-ever Winter Cycling Congress, which took place in Oulu in 2013.

I ask Perälä, whose Twitter bio includes the title 'urban wellbeing engineer', how he became a cyclist.

'In Oulu nobody considers themselves to be a cyclist; I'm not a cyclist! It's just a normal way to get around here,' he answers.

His occupational interest in the field arose in the early 2000s when he was studying civil engineering. On his travels he noticed a curious thing: in many parts of the world, cycling for transportation wasn't a regular part of life.

So he decided to specialise in the field. Today, he's the CEO of Navico, a municipal engineering office that works with the public and private sector on community initiatives and also monitors bicycle path maintenance and determines what types of services should be offered to people in order to encourage year-round cycling.

'Interest in winter cycling is growing all the time in cities around the world,' says Perälä, who also holds the post of cycling coordinator for the city of Oulu, where winter is an eight-month affair and 22 to 27 per cent of cyclists pedal all year round. To that end, 98 per cent of the city's extensive cycling network of 613 kilometres is maintained throughout the year and all routes are always lit.

~

Searching for international comparisons of winter-cycling cultures, I come across a 2016 article in the *Guardian* newspaper by Canadian cycling activist and consultant and designer Anders Swanson. In it, Swanson, a friend and colleague of Perälä's, examines the winter-cycling cultures in different parts of the world. He reports that it's not an easy task, as bike riders under the age of eighteen are not included in some surveys.

Nevertheless, after comparing the numbers he concludes that if Oulu were located in North America, it would be the continent's most bike-friendly city based on its winter-cycling percentage alone, even when compared to the summer-cycling statistics of places such as Portland or Minneapolis, for example.

According to Swanson, in Oulu 30 per cent of children under twelve ride a bicycle to school all year round.

I ask Perälä why Oulu is such a well-functioning winter-cycling city.

He says that part of the reason is because the powers-that-be rejected a car-centric model back in the 1960s.

'Urban planners realised the need for cycling and walking paths here in Oulu,' he replies.

'In successful bicycling cities you can get somewhere directly, whereas with a car you have to circle and navigate a longer route. For example, when new residential areas are built in Oulu, more cycling and walking paths are built than roads. There are also many parks and green areas, so if you're coming from out of town the bike path takes you along the water or through green areas right up to the city centre. It's pleasant and the most practical route – it has to be, because if it's not, people won't use it,' says Perälä.

'City planning in many places doesn't allow for, or encourage, cycling or even walking as a way to get from A to B. But it seems there's growing interest around the world and an effort to change that all the time.'

'An extreme approach – banning cars – doesn't work. A car is good for many things. The best approach is through positivity – not that cars are bad, but that cycling has many environmental and health benefits,' says Perälä.

He says research indicates that about one per cent of people in the world will change their habits for the benefit of the world or for better health – unless they have a heart attack or some medical condition that brings about a change.

'It's all about ease. If the car is the easiest option, then that's what people will likely choose,' says Perälä, who also stresses inclusiveness and access for everyone when it comes to creating the cycling infrastructure. 'Whatever you do you have to make it so that children and the elderly can use it – that should be the benchmark for maintenance, otherwise it's only for the extreme crowd,' he says.

Perälä, the father of a five-year-old, cycles with his daughter all year round and creates and posts videos online to show how easy it can be to pedal in the snow even when temperatures drop below minus 20 degrees Celsius.

'My own daughter has been cycling all year round since she was two. It may take double the time to make a journey with her, but I think it's time well spent as we chat and it's very enjoyable. Of course, it's quite safe here; there's few roads to cross (lots of under- and overpasses) and few hills,' he says.

This is a good example of instilling a sense of practical *sisu* in a young child, while spending some quality time together in the outdoors, getting exercise and encouraging some freedom and independence.

One of my proudest moments as a mum was when my son, without any prompting from me, asked me if he could have winter tyres for his bike so that he could also cycle all year round.

Exercise for everyone

Cycling is also a good form of incidental exercise.

Perälä says: 'For many people the basics are missing, which in many ways is the most important thing. For example, if you're training for a triathlon, you need to maintain your basic fitness level endurance; walking and cycling are great for this. And the easiest way, of course, is daily activity, incidental exercise, that comes without great effort or extra hassle. Diseases such as type 2 diabetes are increasing and it's our sedentary lifestyles, and parents who feel the need to chauffeur children from place to place, that passes on a less active lifestyle to kids.'

'It's good that people play sports and take up other activities, but exercise has been outsourced as something you buy and someone else takes care of,' says Perälä.

I ask him how to encourage people to be more active.

'Little by little, and by trying to get into a routine,' he says. 'If you drive, maybe leave the car a bit further away and then walk. You don't start when it's sleeting out and you need to travel twenty kilometres.'

Perälä has started several local initiatives including *Lähirähinä*, which roughly translates as 'Good for the Hood'. Its goal is to encourage children and parents to participate in different sports activities in their community. 'It started to bother me immensely that parents would drive their kids to sports or hobbies and then sit there tapping away on their mobile while the kids played. Then they get in the car and drive home and that was their "together" time,' says Perälä.

'The pace of modern life is quite hectic – a car is a good aid, but I think it's taken over too much of life. And it's worrisome how much screen time children have. There's no point in forbidding screen time; we can use technology to aid movement and to instigate group activity, for example playing games indoors using digitally interactive floors and walls that encourage people to move.

'So many of our problems we create ourselves,' he says, echoing what I firmly believe.

Along with the health and environmental benefits of choosing biking over driving, my friend Tiina sees another upside.

'I think that when people spend a lot of time in their cars, they're separated from society, humanity and the world,' says Tiina, who also views using public transit as a way to stay real.

'Sure, if you sit in a tram or a bus, there may occasionally be a drunk or someone less than pleasant to contend with, but you're participating in the world in the same way that you are when you're on your bike. You're seeing people and experiencing the environment. You're not in an isolated metal box,' says Tiina, who cycles all year round.

She uses the family car she shares with her husband about once every two weeks to take care of several errands in one go or travel to the cottage.

There's a social element to pedalling, as I'm part of the landscape. I wave to friends and neighbours and even stop for a chat, if I have time, when I see someone I know.

Our friend Riikka also shares our enthusiasm and addiction for cycling, especially during the winter months.

'Winter cycling is just like skiing or some form of practical exercise. Once you're hooked, it's hard to take public transport,' says Riikka. Even though her family also owns a car, she uses her bicycle as it's much easier and faster than driving to her workplace, which is about two and a half kilometres away.

'People ask if I'm cold when I cycle during the winter, but I'm actually warmer because I'm moving more than if I were standing and waiting for a tram,' she says. 'As long as you've got sensible clothing, like weather-proof outdoor pants and a proper coat and gloves, it's really quite easy to do. Though maybe it's not so feminine,' she says.

For the record, I've seen Riikka cycling during the winter wearing a skirt and wool tights and looking quite elegant.

In fact, part of the bicycling lifestyle was one of the things that drew Riikka and her family to sell their house out in the countryside and opt for a smaller, more centrally located apartment.

'When we lived out in the country in a large house we ended up driving a lot, even though the idea was that we would be close to nature. The reality was that I was using the car all the time and didn't really bike anywhere because the distances were long – the grocery store alone was eight kilometres away,' she says.

'I really wanted to return to the city for a more functional lifestyle. When we moved back here I became much more active.'

Katja Pantzar

The joy of biking

Aside from cycling's health benefits, one of the main reasons that I choose to pedal is simple: it makes me feel happy.

Over the years I've read an array of books that explore various human emotions – from Gretchen Rubin's *The Happiness Project* to Andrew Solomon's *The Noonday Demon: An Atlas of Depression*. I also do yoga, which I enjoy, and tried meditation, which admittedly I'm not very good at.

I seem to find my inner peace through movement and reading.

From charting my own quest to feel better and by observing the numerous ways that people try to achieve happiness, my takeaway is that a great many people find joy in a relatively simple, healthy and balanced lifestyle, coupled with supportive friends and family, and a sense of purpose whether through meaningful work or activities that makes them feel worthwhile and part of a community.

I'm not a philosopher and it would be foolhardy for me to say that I've figured out the how of happiness because it means so many different things to different people. Besides, very highly qualified people who have studied the topic for years have written volumes and volumes on it.

When the World Happiness Report was published in 2017 – it features happiness scores averaged between the years of 2014 and 2016 from 155 countries – Finland came in fifth, after Nordic neighbours Norway, Denmark and Iceland. Switzerland was in fourth place.

Among the metrics used were access to high-quality social support networks, healthy years of life expectancy and freedom to make life decisions, for example.

Now, if you were to land in Helsinki in the middle of winter and take a tram with a group of stony-faced Finns, you might wonder what on earth the ranking was based on.

If I were to generalise, I would say that while Finns can seem reserved at first, a shyness that might even be misinterpreted as rudeness – especially in regions where there's not a culture of making small talk with people you don't know – part of that restraint is actually a respect for other people's space.

Once you've managed to break the ice, which is not very hard to do, I've found that most Finns are incredibly warm, kind and friendly.

When I first arrived in Finland, I asked a colleague why Finns didn't smile much. She considered my question for a moment and then replied: 'They're smiling on the inside.'

Initially, I didn't understand her answer. But over time I've come to interpret the quietness and introversion as a cultural norm or characteristic that I've encountered in some other countries in northern Europe. Here, walking around smiling and telling people how great you feel or how fabulously things are going for you is simply not the done thing. But this has an upside, which is that feeling melancholy is socially acceptable.

That means there's less pressure to appear happy. Tove Jansson's loveable Moomins embrace an undertone of melancholy – they occasionally have a good cry and accept that life's ups and downs are part of the package – and that's okay.

Here, I am accepted as, sometimes, melancholy me.

Happiness through living, not searching

I've also noticed that in focusing on finding meaning in nature, physical activity, family, friends, learning and work, I've inadvertently found a place of contentment.

In Michael Moore's 2015 *Where to Invade Next* documentary, the award-winning American writer and director travels to countries around the world that excel in specific areas ranging from healthcare to sex and equality.

Moore stops in Finland to uncover the secrets of what makes the education system so successful and meets with a group of teachers at a Helsinki primary school. A lively discussion ensues about the differences between the American and Finnish systems. One of the Finnish teachers says: 'School is about finding your happiness, finding a way to learn what makes you happy.' That line stays with me.

In educational expert Pasi Sahlberg's *Finnish Lessons 2.0*, he holds that literacy is part of the key to joy when he describes the Finnish classic Aleksis Kivi's *Seven Brothers* from 1870: 'It is a story of orphan brothers who realise that becoming literate is the key to happiness and a good life.'

Sahlberg goes on to write: 'Since those days, reading has been an integral part of Finnish culture. Education has served as the main strategy for building a literate society and a nation that is today known by the world for its cultural and technological achievements.'

Finland ranks as the world's most literate nation and holds some of the highest library-book-borrowing figures in the world.

Here, everyone seems to read: newspapers, books, magazines, and regardless of their walk of life. In the excellent public library system that brims with books in a range of languages, I often find the latest international English-language titles. There's also a vibrant literary scene that hosts events and readings for the public at no cost. Over the years I've listened to interviews at local bookshops with renowned authors ranging from writer and director Paul Auster to bestselling and award-winning authors such as Donna Tartt, Naomi Klein, Michael Cunningham and Aravind Adiga, to name but a few.

There's a Finnish saying, '*Onni ei tule etsien, vaan eläen*', which means, 'Happiness is not found by searching but by living.' To that I would add, 'and by reading and cycling'.

For reading and cycling can be done either alone or together with friends. And both activities help to develop *sisu* – one by challenging the mind with new ideas and journeys of thought and concentration, the other by stimulating the body physically through movement and travel. Both can help to refresh the mind and open up new landscapes and horizons, internal and external.

Happiness is not found by searching but by living.

Cycling *sisu*

- *Pedalling addresses a range of issues, from countering the effects of a sedentary lifestyle to elevating mood, providing stress relief, and boosting creativity and brain power.*
- *Can you use cycling as a form of transport? It may actually save time and money.*
- *Build up a standard kit of what you need: a helmet, raingear, lights and reflectors; once you have all the basic equipment, it's easier to make it into a daily or weekly habit.*
- *Keep it enjoyable, it doesn't have to be a triathlon – even a few kilometres a day, or a week, is great.*
- *Find a cycling friend: when you agree to meet up with someone it can make it easier and more enjoyable to pedal.*
- *In places where cycling as a form of transport is not an option, consider other alternatives such as nearby woods or local parks that have bicycle paths or lanes.*

CHAPTER 9

The benefits of movement as medicine (and incidental exercise)

~~~~~

Growing up, I was accustomed to the idea that pills – whether over-the-counter or prescription – were the quick fix to just about every problem, physical or psychological.

That attitude still prevails. Just watching American television for an hour leaves me convinced that I could have a staggering range of medical conditions that I didn't even know existed, all of which could be cured with the right pill. The high usage of prescription drugs in North

America, such as opioids – often prescribed for chronic pain – is part of the reason for the opioid crisis. The US and Canada were ranked first and second respectively for per capita opioid use in 2016, according to the United Nations International Narcotics Control Board.

During my North American years, I took a range of prescription pills and over-the-counter medicine. From painkillers and the antibiotics that I was prescribed as a teenager to clear up acne, to the antidepressants that helped pull me out of a serious bout of depression when I was first diagnosed in my twenties. I also regularly took anti-anxiety medication in my late twenties and early thirties, as prescribed by a doctor.

I don't doubt the benefits of medicine in pill form – it's up to an individual and their medical practitioner to decide and I have definitely benefitted from a low dose of antidepressants at difficult points during my adult life. But before I moved to the Nordics it hadn't occured to me that I might deal with physical pain, such as headaches or cramps, or emotional pain, such as feeling depressed or anxious, in ways other than by taking a pill – or pulling the covers over my head.

That gradual realisation that I might actually be able to do something concrete came through the discovery of two

key concepts that just about every Finn seems to know –
liike on lääke (movement is medicine) and *hyötyliikunta* or
incidental exercise.

But before discovering these concepts, I found myself in
a surprising situation that started the process of thinking
about other ways that I might address physical or mental
pain.

~~~

A few months after I moved to Finland in the early 2000s, I
went for my new employee health check-up. The goal was
to rate my overall health and wellbeing, as well as to meet
with an occupational therapist to assess whether I was
executing the optimal sitting or standing posture at my
workstation.

Naturally, I took my prescriptions from Canada with me,
assuming they would be renewed. My security blanket was
an anti-anxiety medication that I had been taking regularly to
deal with general life stress relating to issues such as work, a
long-distance relationship and moving countries, which at
the time was intended to be temporary, for a year or so.

I sat in the doctor's office and we reviewed my general
health and eventually got around to the medication part. I

was surprised to hear the doctor say that my anti-anxiety prescription was considered highly addictive. Instead of approving an instant renewal, the doctor suggested that I look into more natural remedies such as mild exercise or talk therapy to address the underlying issues causing the anxiety. I'm told that if I really want a prescription for a different type of anxiety medication, I can have one. But the question is posed: would it be possible to try some other options before choosing the pill form?

As I sat there, I realised that owing to the high amount of exercise and fresh air that I've got during my first few months – some simply from riding my bike to and from work – and my slightly more balanced lifestyle, I've actually taken much less of those meds.

Although the terror of not having my security blanket in pill form is great, I decide to give it a try.

Incidentally, a doctor *not* immediately prescribing anti-anxiety medication is something I've experienced on several occasions in Finland. Different doctors on various occasions have suggested talk therapy or exercise as healthier options, and have taken the time to speak to me about the side effects and possible problems of anti-anxiety medication, especially for someone prone to depression.

This is not to say that people in Finland don't take prescription drugs and medicines such as anti-anxiety meds (they do), but my experiences here help me to start rethinking what medicines I take. Eventually, through using movement and exercise to reduce my dose, I reach the point where I no longer take anti-anxiety medicine and take significantly fewer painkillers.

Despite the top quality-of-life rankings, many people in Finland, as in so many other parts of the world, suffer from depression, too.

According to Finland's National Institute for Health and Welfare, '1 in 5 Finns will suffer from depression during their lifetime.' For comparison, according to the Mental Health Commission of Canada, 1 in 5 people in Canada experience a mental health problem or illness.

The source of my sadness

Over time I have come to understand that the roots of my depression lie in many things. I believe it's partly just the way I'm 'wired'. I also seem to lack a toughness filter and can be overly sensitive to the woes of the world. When I'm feeling low, just walking past someone on the street who is clearly down and out, perhaps homeless, can set my mind off into a downward spiral of wondering and worrying about what happened to that man or woman who was once someone's baby, someone's child.

I can also be very hard on myself and need to constantly challenge the notion I have that I'm not good enough. I have a tendency to ruminate, worry and speculate about worst-case scenarios, which are also common to states of anxiety and depression.

For much of my childhood, adolescence and early adulthood, I longed to fit in and be like everyone else – whatever that meant.

It is only as an adult in my forties that I have come to accept myself as I am: an outsider, who is neither from here nor there. And that can actually be an asset. It means that I can feel at home in many different places from India to Iceland and write my own life script, so to speak. Having an outsider's perspective has also been advantageous professionally because it gives me the ability to see issues from several different angles.

A major turning point was accepting that my depression is an illness, a condition that I can manage through lifestyle choices. I won't be magically cured, but when I'm stressed or feeling gloomy because I think that I haven't done a good enough job at home or work, I need to gather up my

Finnish resilience, tap into that *sisu*, and take action. That means when I feel tired or achy, doing something as simple as going for a short walk along the tree-lined shore or taking a quick dip in the sea can stop my downward spiral from developing into something more serious.

Movement as medicine

The first of the two concepts that I become acquainted with that helps me reduce the medicine I take and move away from the idea that I need to have a complicated or costly fitness routine to stay healthy is the idea of movement as medicine (*liike on lääke* in Finnish).

The movement as medicine idea holds that physical activity can help a person maintain better overall wellbeing and health by helping to prevent or manage certain conditions. For example, for some people, prolonged tension of shoulder and neck muscles can lead to a headache. Some may benefit from stretching and strengthening these muscles as a way to alleviate pain and to possibly even help prevent the onset or frequency of headaches.

Regular physical activity, even something as simple as going for a short walk several times a week, choosing to take the stairs instead of the elevator, or taking regular breaks at work to do some gentle arm circles or overhead stretches, can be beneficial for muscle, joint and bone health, as well as improve circulation, which is necessary to counter a sedentary lifestyle.

Variations of this idea exist in many other cultures and date back to ancient times. However, in Finland everyone seems to be familiar with the concept as a kind of folk wisdom. As part of my cultural immersion, I start to become aware of how movement, even a little bit, can make a huge difference. I come to realise that I don't need to embark on a hardcore fitness programme in order to improve my overall fitness and wellbeing. Every day I can make a few easy, simple choices that are beneficial.

I become aware of how movement, even a little bit, can make a huge difference.

Incidental exercise

The other concept that most Finns seem to know and embrace is the idea of incidental exercise (hyötyliikunta in Finnish), which is carried out several times a week and often even daily. It's physical activity that is not exercise per se. For example, cleaning, biking or walking to work, shovelling snow, raking leaves, chopping wood, playing with a child or climbing up stairs are all considered good forms of incidental exercise.

My icy dips are a good example of movement as medicine. Some mornings or evenings, I only have time for a very short dip in the sea – one minute or less. I'm not swimming lengths or having an extreme workout. But that movement, along with the benefits of the cold water, is enough to address issues ranging from tiredness to sore muscles or tense neck and shoulders, which can escalate into a headache if not dealt with. Instead of first reaching for a pill, I experiment with going for an invigorating dip when I have an ache or pain in my body or mind. And most of the time it does the trick.

There are, of course, many people and schools of thought around the world that know that movement and exercise can address a range of health issues. But for me, this is a life-changing realisation: I can do something relatively time-efficient and cost-free and dramatically change how I'm feeling physically and mentally.

My wise friend Tiina also uses the movement as medicine technique.

'If I have a cramp or a pain, I first treat it with movement. And then if it doesn't go away, I'll consider massage, acupuncture or physio. But I don't go to a doctor or reach for painkillers first, especially if it's a stiffness or cramp that I think is a natural part of ageing,' she says. 'Of course, if it's something more serious, then it's necessary to go to the doctor.'

I think that healthy approach to accepting the aches and pains that come with ageing is also part of the sensible Nordic approach.

The other problem with taking a lot of medication, of course, is the side effects. This is well known and well documented, but it's not until I revamp my lifestyle that I realise how many of the medications I was taking were working at cross-purposes.

For example, the sleeping pills that I took at one point to battle insomnia, would knock me out at night, but I would wake feeling groggy and a sluggishness would stay with me during the day. In an effort to boost my low energy levels, I ate more sugary snacks, which in turn led to weight gain. Those extra kilos made me feel pudgy and down, as my clothes became too tight.

While many people suffering from insomnia benefit from a short dose of sleeping pills (myself included), a much better option for me was adopting lifestyle habits that included more movement and activity outdoors during the daytime to ensure that in the evening I was physically tired in a natural way and therefore better able to fall asleep and sleep well – naturally.

In hindsight, this seems so simple and so obvious.

Health-enhancing activities

As awareness of the importance of movement and exercise grows, around the world health organisations are recommending physical activity to address a range of health issues.

In Finland, the national Care Guidelines, 'independent, evidence-based clinical practice guidelines', cover important issues related to health and medical treatment as well as prevention of disease. Regular exercise is recommended in the prevention, treatment and rehabilitation of a range of illnesses, including depression.

There's also an institute devoted to promoting health-enhancing physical activity. Called the UKK Institute, one of its main mandates is to 'develop effective research-based practices that help reduce sedentary behaviour and promote health-enhancing physical activity'.

The private research institute is named after Finland's longest-serving president Urho Kaleva Kekkonen (1900–1986) who was in power from 1956 to 1982. In addition to Kekkonen's political achievements, he was an active sportsman and high-jump champion.

UKK National Park, named after the statesman, is one of the country's largest protected natural areas; it sits near the top of the country in Lapland and includes the Kiilopää area and its peak.

According to the Institute, incidental exercise – such as playing with a child, and carrying out household chores such as cleaning or foraging – has many benefits ranging from reducing the risk of developing coronary artery disease, cardiovascular disease and type 2 diabetes to slowing down the development of osteoporosis and easing symptoms of depression and anxiety.

As my interest in movement and incidental exercise grows, I happen to notice that one of UKK's major seminars is called 'Movement is Medicine' and features a range of top speakers from doctors and researchers to occupational health experts.

I immediately sign up for the two-day seminar.

On the first day of the seminar, almost as soon as I settle into my seat in the packed auditorium, we're told to stand up. In keeping with the event's theme there are group stretches in between presentations.

As everyone now knows, sitting is the new smoking.

Though I'm unable to stay for the entire session, two things stand out. One, everyone present appears fit and energetic. But it follows that if you have an interest, professional or otherwise, in the field and are carrying a message about the benefits of movement, you are more likely to practise what you preach.

The second theme I notice is that although several apps and technology innovations for aiding people with incorporating more movement into their lives are highlighted, the main message is that simple and sensible movement and activity and moderation are the solution to so many health problems that plague people everywhere.

A 2016 study published by the peer-reviewed medical journal *The Lancet* of more than one million people found that physical inactivity costs the world economy more than 56 billion euros a year in healthcare costs, and a sedentary lifestyle is linked to an increase in type 2 diabetes, heart disease and some cancers.

One seminar about the key to a good night's sleep interests me. I later go online to read the abstract. The author Heli Järnefelt, a specialist psychologist with the Finnish Institute of Occupational Health, emphasises that the first choice is to find a pill-free treatment. While her paper outlines different ways, including various forms of cognitive behaviour therapy to meditation and mindfulness, to help address the underlying issues causing sleeplessness, she also points out that those underlying issues can be lifestyle factors, such as inactivity and too much internet or game time before or instead of going to sleep.

One of the movement is medicine founding fathers in Finland is professor emeritus and medical doctor Ilkka Vuori, who is often called the 'father of health-enhancing physical activity'. (His title sounds better in Finnish.)

Vuori was the first director of the UKK Institute, a post he held for twenty years. During his career he's been a visiting professor at Stanford University, published more than 350 articles in medical journals and written numerous books. He has contributed to research and health-related policymaking with a wide range of organisations in Finland and abroad, including the WHO and HEPA, the WHO's European network for the promotion of health-enhancing physical activity.

I meet the dapper octogenarian at a café housed in an Art Nouveau building in Porvoo, one of Finland's six picturesque medieval towns.

I ask Vuori about the roots of the movement as medicine idea, which a great many people seem to be familiar with.

'There are many reasons for this familiarity,' he says. 'In the last hundred years Finland has developed from a very poor country to a prosperous one; movement was a necessity for a long time. Up to the 1960s and 1970s, cars were not as common in Finland as they were in, say, America,' he says. 'So going to work, school, running errands was done by walking or bicycling. Nowadays, although just about everyone owns a car or a motorcycle, an active approach to life has been preserved here,' he says.

According to Vuori, the active approach has remained in part due to tradition and part because it's a practical way of life that neatly serves several purposes; for example, gathering mushrooms and berries or chopping wood for the sauna while spending time outdoors and getting some fresh air and activity.

There's also the element of the national character.

'Finns prefer to manage and take care of their own affairs; some services that could be outsourced and purchased haven't developed here. For example, there are hundreds of thousands of summer cottages in Finland, but there are very few summer cottage caretakers; it's a service that's only come up in the last few years. This indicates that people want to take care of their cottages on their own. And they enjoy doing that,' he explains.

(This sounds like a perfect example of the do-it-yourself *sisu* that I observed early on, with people *choosing* to carry out household and other tasks that could have been easily outsourced.)

Vuori says these foundations, a Nordic practicality, are coupled with a very strong sports culture facilitated by numerous local and national organisations that organise different sports, which means that almost everyone who has grown up in Finland has participated in sports as a child.

Physicians who prescribed moderate exercise or movement for their patients include Hippocrates of Greece and Susruta of India, according to 'The History of Exercise is Medicine in Ancient Civilizations', a 2014 article in the American Physiological Society's *Advances in Physiology Education*.

Almost everyone who has grown up in Finland has participated in sports as a child.

In the modern-day context, Vuori credits Jerry Morris, a Scottish epidemiologist who is widely acknowledged for discovering the link between sedentary behaviour and cardiovascular disease. In the late 1940s and early 1950s Morris studied and compared the health of London bus drivers who sat while working to bus conductors who walked up and down the stairs during their shift. Morris discovered that the conductors who moved at work had a lower incidence of cardiovascular disease.

Over the years, Vuori has worked with many people on the international scene who have been instrumental in studying the health-enhancing properties of movement and physical activity, such as Dr Steven Blair, an American professor and exercise scientist, who devoted his career to studying and encouraging people to move. Another is Dr Victor KR Matsudo, who started the Agita Mundo movement in São Paulo, which became the International Society for Physical Activity and Health.

Vuori, who spent the early years of his medical career as a sports doctor and was the Finnish Olympic team's doctor at the 1968 Mexico Olympics, says that it's been a long journey convincing the medical profession and policy makers of the benefits of movement.

'The effects and benefits of being in shape have always been known, but it took a very long time for the health effects of movement to be accepted. In medicine there's a healthy scepticism toward adopting new or preventative forms of treatment that have not been scientifically proven,' he says.

'In 1987 I published a piece in the *Finnish Medical Journal* that posed the question: is walking fitness? Many of my colleagues at the time came to ask me, somewhat incredulously, if it really was possible to improve your fitness and health by just walking. The answer was and is "yes",' he says.

Vuori says he's delighted to see how far the field of movement is medicine has come over the past fifty or sixty years.

'The big wheels have started turning at the policy level in different countries and internationally. A good example of this is the WHO's 2017 development of a draft global plan of action to promote physical activity, which is a first,' he says.

The WHO has identified lack of physical activity as the fourth leading cause of morbidity.

As for Vuori, he practises what he preaches. One of his favourite activities is 'summerhouse DIY', which he tells me includes chopping wood, fishing, taking care of the garden and mowing the lawn. He also enjoys skiing and walks in the woods for almost an hour every day.

I ask him whether he has advice for people who struggle to incorporate movement into their daily lives. He thinks for a moment and replies: 'Don't try to come up with ways to avoid daily movement and activity – at home, work, commuting to work or during leisure time. Use any opportunity, even if it's for a short time and it's light movement,' he says.

'What's indisputable is that even some kind of movement is better than none at all. Maintaining functional capacity and mobility are key for quality of life and for managing health,' he adds.

DIY *sisu*

When it comes to incidental exercise – physical activity that takes place while you're ostensibly doing something else – there's often a playful, pragmatic approach in the local press about ways to liven up and maximise the effect of carrying out basic household or yard chores. For example, three shoulder stretches with a rake following a session of sweeping up autumn leaves.

Many people I meet share this logical approach to incidental exercise, and part of their DIY-*sisu* spirit translates into enjoying a variety of tasks that might be more easily outsourced, as occurs in other countries where a culture of convenience prevails.

A good example comes from two of my fellow winter swimmers, a charming couple, Timo and Pia, who are both retired pilots.

Timo, who often jovially dances a post-swim jig on the dock, and his wife Pia go for a dip together every morning during the winter swimming season.

One day we are talking about swimming, sauna and that special Finnish quality of resilience.

'*Sisu* is when you discover your own strength. It comes from perseverance and hard conditions – historically Finns had to go out on the farm, or to the barn, or fishing, regardless of the weather,' says Timo.

Then he tells me that cleaning (yes, good old-fashioned house or apartment tidying up), a form of incidental exercise, is a *sisu*-building activity for him.

Of course it would be easier to hire a cleaner, as many

people do, but Timo says he enjoys the challenge: 'You set yourself up to carry out the task and it just makes you feel so good when you've done it,' he says.

They tell me that they started one of their other *sisu*-building activities, winter swimming, fifteen years ago when they were both still working flying planes around Europe and places further afield. 'We got so hooked on it that we used to go for a dip before an early morning flight so as to be full of energy,' says Pia.

But their secret to staying healthy is simple: 'Exercise is a way of life that we've been doing together for thirty years.'

The outdoor gym

Incidental exercise doesn't replace proper fitness training; ideally a person should do both, though this of course depends on age and health.

Certainly there are people in Finland with personal trainers and intense fitness programmes, but there seems to be a general acceptance of a practical, less-is-more philosophy when it comes to movement.

When I adopt this approach, it helps me to consider other exercise options, as I no longer feel that improving my level of fitness and strength means that I need to join a gym or sign up for an intense, hard-core exercise programme that needs to be followed to a T.

In the spring of 2016 I go for a regular health check-up at our local public health centre.

As I sit there in my bra during my physical, the young doctor and I review my general health habits, which he says are good.

But then he looks at my arms and shoulders, and suggests that I might consider strengthening and toning my upper body muscles through lifting weights or some other type of muscle strengthening and toning programme. This might also help to reduce the headaches and migraines that I occasionally suffer, which I believe are brought on in part by neck and shoulder muscle tension, likely the result of too many hours spent hunched over a computer.

By this point I've been in Finland for so long that I'm used to and appreciate the honest, direct, non-sugar-coated Finnish delivery. Because I know that what he says is true. I just needed someone to tell me.

Though the doctor suggests a strength-training programme at a gym, I don't like the idea of spending any more time indoors.

Given that I don't have a lot of extra time in between juggling family, a young child and a busy freelance career, I start thinking about what I might do that would keep me outdoors and could be done before my family wakes up.

When I was young, about ten or so, I did some sports such as gymnastics and track and field. But being pushed to run competitively at elementary school left me strongly disliking running, and I vowed to never do it again.

Yet, as I review my options from a Nordic practicality perspective, it seems that of all my options, the most simple and sensible would be to incorporate a light morning jog into my schedule and combine it with some basic sit-ups and push-ups.

Which is how I found myself heading out for my first run in almost twenty-five years one spring morning and discovering that my general level of fitness is poorer than I thought. Although I stretch before I head out on that first run, the whole experience hurts and feels almost impossible, not just during the few minutes that I manage to jog, but afterwards when every muscle in my body aches.

But somehow I persevere – I tap into that reserve of *sisu* that I found with winter swimming and remember how pushing beyond the discomfort was key to getting to a better, stronger and more comfortable place.

The first few times I manage to run for about three minutes before having to stop and walk the rest of the way. But as it's spring and the mornings are light and bright, I continue, telling myself that even five minutes of running are beneficial and better than nothing.

Sure enough, within a few weeks, it no longer hurts to run and I gradually increase the distance. My goal is not a marathon, great speed or long distances, but just to work up a sweat, get a bit of cardio, and tone up my muscles with a few exercises before I head for the water.

Within a month, I'm hooked. My mini-jogs as I call them are about ten to fifteen minutes long and a few times a week I run along the shorefront path of our island before stopping at the rug-washing dock to do a few exercises and then plopping into the sea.

I take inspiration from my fellow winter swimmers, who move to the nearby dock when the winter swimming club closes in early spring, and continue the practice of going for a daily transformative dip all year round.

In order to build up my muscle strength, I start incorporating some basic plank-style push-ups against the railings of the dock along with some very elementary sit-ups. At first I can barely do a set of five or ten without feeling completely spent. But within a month or two, I can do a set of sixty or eighty crunches without collapsing.

When the water warms up to about 15 degrees Celsius, I figure out a way to do a type of chin-up hanging from the railing on the wooden dock and lifting my body in and out of the water. As with the sit-ups and push-ups, I can barely do five when I start.

But relatively quickly my endurance improves and I'm able to progress to ten chin-ups, then fifteen, then twenty, and then twenty-five.

I've turned the rug-washing dock into an outdoor gym.

I realise that my new routine requires a proper backpack suitable for running that can accommodate a towel, change of clothes and water bottle.

Again, I do something that I've not done since I was a teenager – I buy a proper sports backpack with straps at the waist and chest. This is possibly the first time as an adult that I haven't chosen a bag based on its brand name or look: this one is chosen purely for function.

My new jogging habit improves my cardio, increases muscle tone and strengthens my upper body, which admittedly was becoming flabby and rounded from years of being hunched over a computer and, to be honest, from age. Thankfully, my new workout habit soon helps to lessen the number of headaches I get.

When the icy winter months arrive, I buy some spikes that strap onto my shoes so that I continue running, whatever the weather.

Though I don't have any triathlon aspirations, my new exercise routine significantly boosts my wellbeing – I feel stronger after I do it. Some might question its efficacy given its relatively short length. But on the days that I carry it out, I get a good half an hour or so of exercise. Combined with my cycling, I'm getting at least an hour or more of exercise or movement in a way that's relatively easy to fit into my day.

My new habit also helps me to develop something that *sisu* expert Emilia Lahti refers to as 'life insurance' – by taking care of your own physical wellbeing you also strengthen your mind and your self.

When Lahti and I were discussing whether being physically strong increases *sisu*, I asked about her own running, which is admittedly on a completely different level to mine.

She told me she first discovered running when she was twenty-two, and it was a surprise because she'd never considered herself a good athlete. 'In school I was always picked last for the sports team,' she says.

'I randomly went for a run and ran for forty minutes and my mind was blown. Previously, I had struggled with running but that run triggered something in me: I signed up and did my first marathon six months later.

'Later it emerged as this organic thing. I can honestly attribute my sanity to the fact that I have running. For me, running allowed me to feel strong again in my mind and heart,' she says.

'When I train, it's more than me just strengthening my ligaments, or my aerobic fitness; during those hours it's almost like my body is telling my mind: you can do this. Every time I go back I remember that I can do it.'

'There's some kind of power circuit or a phenomenon that happens when we physically move that changes something in our minds and not necessarily the other way around. We're so obsessed with having the mind control and the mental power but for a person who is depressed – I've been depressed so I know first-hand – you don't want to get out of bed. It's like the body is in a deep sleep and it literally can't get up. If you do manage to somehow get out of bed and into the shower, it almost gives you an energy boost.'

Despite my admiration for Emilia Lahti's ultra-marathons it is the non-competitive nature of so many of the activities that I have undertaken here in the north that appeals to me.

This non-competitive quality that I have tapped into ties into a contentedness that I have found in so many pursuits. For although winning is important for Finns, especially in an ice hockey match against your most important rival Sweden, it's not about aiming for the top spot, but rather about ensuring that you do a good job and enjoy it.

When a fellow winter swimmer suggests that I consider participating in the Ice Swimming Championships, I seriously consider it. I look up the event online and browse travel and accommodation options. And think about how I might train for it.

But then, in the water (naturally) I have the realisation that one of the reasons I enjoy winter swimming so much is because it's not a competition.

This affirms my decision not to sign up for the competition. One of the many reasons I love my polar practice is because I don't have to prove anything to anyone.

And it's the same with my newfound jogging and exercise programme. At the end of the day, it's not about how fast, how far, or how many push-ups or sit-ups I can chalk up, it's about having a strong body that is relatively pain-free and works and feels good and can pedal up a hill without becoming breathless. Or pick up my son and carry him – even as he grows and tips the scale at over twenty-five kilograms.

I am accepted as I am, I learn to accept myself and however well I do is fine.

Movement as medicine

'Use any opportunity, even if it's for a short time and features light movement. Don't try to come up with ways to avoid daily movement and activity at home, work, commuting to work, or in free time.'

Professor emeritus and movement as medicine expert Ilkka Vuori.

- *Try using movement to relieve muscle tension, stiffness or stress by going for a short walk.*
- *Supplement household chores or yard work such as mowing the lawn with easy stretches.*
- *Schedule a walking meeting instead of sitting down.*
- *If you want to measure your progress and set goals, use a pedometer to monitor your daily activity.*
- *Movement and exercise help to build health and stamina, which leads to more sisu.*

CHAPTER 10

Nordic minimalism: creating a simpler and more sustainable lifestyle

Early one summer morning I walk towards the sea along the tree-lined gravel footpath flanking the shoreline where the pale yellow icebreakers, including *Sisu*, named after that unique form of fortitude and resilience, are docked.

When I reach the dock, a woman in her late sixties who I recognise from our swimming circles is scrubbing a traditional rag rug with a brush and some pine soap on one of the wooden tables. We greet one another and chat briefly about the water – it's still fairly cool at 17 degrees Celsius – and the weather, which is bright and sunny despite the early hour.

After a short swim, I climb back up the metal ladder onto the dock. As I'm towelling myself off, I step over to admire the pure reds, blues and greens of the rag rug, which is woven from strips of recycled fabric.

The woman lights up as she tells me the rug's story. As a child more than half a century ago, she watched her mother make the rug on a loom. Pointing to a section of red, she tells me it's from one of her mother's old aprons. The bright blue portion was once part of her father's old work uniform. And the green fabric came from a pair of sports trousers she wore as a young girl until she outgrew them.

She tells me that as time goes by she cherishes the heirloom more and more. 'Every day it's as though I'm walking through my family history,' she says.

As we stand there on the sunlit dock, the natural scent of pine wafting in the air, I think to myself that that rag rug represents a perfect example of Nordic practicality – recasting something old into a new item that serves a purpose and carries a meaningful story.

A new approach

I came of age at a time in the late '80s and early '90s when conspicuous consumption was cool. Buying stuff was an activity, a pastime, even a sport in the spirit of the popular idiom: shop till you drop.

Yet I notice here in Finland, as in some other parts of northern Europe, showy materialism and an excessive display of possessions are almost frowned upon. If you happen to own a big house and a flashy car and a summer cottage in the archipelago that's fine, but it's not something to brag about or constantly refer to. The same goes for designer clothing and accessories.

Initially I consider this pared-down approach to be part of the Nordic lifestyle. As people tend to live in relatively small apartments and houses, having less stuff is also a necessity.

But as I learn more about the country's design legacy, I come to understand that there's much more to Nordic minimalism – the idea that less is more – than merely a decluttered style aesthetic.

Nordic minimalism – the idea that less is more.

Finnish design is renowned around the world for its timeless minimalist lines and functionality.

I was familiar with design icons such as Marimekko, with their fabulous bold prints in clothing, accessories and home wares, and those ubiquitous orange-handled Fiskars scissors, which are reportedly the world's bestseller.

But what I had not properly understood was one of the philosophies underlining it all: that one well-made, sustainably and ethically produced functional item will stand the test of time over several cheap, poor-quality or unethically made products that will need to be thrown out and replaced.

A few select examples of this include works by the great architect and designer Alvar Aalto (1898–1976) such as the iconic Aalto Vase created in 1936 which continues to sell from London to Buenos Aires. The undulating form of the glass vase mimics waves, which is also what *aalto* means in Finnish.

Kartio drinking glasses are another good example. Designed by Kaj Franck in 1958, the classic tumblers come in a range of shades from apple green to sea blue, rain, emerald, and ultramarine blue, and have been a staple of design-savvy homes since their inception.

Yet another of Aalto's iconic creations, the Artek Stool E60 launched by the modernist master in 1933, represents an excellent example of form follows function. The three-legged modern classic made of birch veneer has been copied endlessly since its debut more than half a century ago. But an authentic E60 stool is intended to last forever. And it can be dressed up or down, stacked in the corner of a room to save space, or used as a coffee table, bookstand or nightstand. The stackable seats are re-sold and re-sold, maintaining and even exceeding their original value at times.

Two quotes by Alvar Aalto sum up his philosophy, which could also be considered general principles of Finnish design: 'Form must have a content, and that content must be linked to nature', and 'Beauty is the harmony of purpose and form.'

The democracy of design

Where I once practised retail therapy as a pick-me-up, I've learnt a new approach to acquiring clothing and accessories, even household items for that matter, which is that all of my purchases should have a function and serve a purpose.

At its heart, the Finnish design ideology represents a sustainable ethic. By investing in a good stool or vase or drinking glass you don't need to keep buying new ones. Though it may require a bit more of an investment initially, in the long run it's easier on the wallet and the environment.

There's a Finnish saying *Köyhällä ei ole varaa ostaa halpaa*, which roughly translates to 'The poor cannot afford to buy cheap.'

Whereas 'design' and 'designer' can equal exclusivity in some parts of the world, Finnish design embodies the ideas of equality and access for everyone that are so prominent in many areas of life in Finland from education to exercise.

Finnish design embodies the ideas of equality and access for everyone that are so prominent in many areas of life in Finland.

I come to think of this equality as democracy of design: design is intended for everyone as a way to improve the quality of daily life. And it's not merely about objects – it's an approach to life, whether it's the creation of a functional city tram with a section for infant prams to be parked safely and neatly in the carriage so they don't block the doors; the lighting of a trail in the middle of a forested section of a city park so that people can go for a walk or a jog when it's dark; or the functionality of a public service provider's website that operates in a logical, user-friendly manner. Design is meant for everyone and strives for easy usability for everyone.

While there are many high-tech examples of Finnish design, two classic examples of everyday design are the dish-drying cupboard and the humble pedestrian reflector.

The dish-drying cupboard was developed by Maiju Gebhard for the Finnish Association of Work Efficiency (what a name!) in the mid-1940s to eliminate manual drying of dishes. It's built into the kitchen cupboard above the sink, so that after dishes are hand washed they can be placed in the slots to dry. The space saver, which has an aesthetic component – drying dishes are out of sight – represents a good example of form follows function, not to mention sustainability: no oil or electricity needed. Despite the prevalence of dishwashing machines, many Finnish kitchens still include a dish-drying cupboard today, which is handy for fragile items that can't be machine-washed and for small households.

Another brilliant example of Finnish design is the safety reflector, which was created by Arvi Lehti in the 1950s, initially to protect cars and horse carriages and then later adapted for pedestrian use.

Today safety reflectors are available in an array of colours and shapes designed as an accessory that can be attached to a coat or bag, for example, to ensure that a pedestrian or cyclist is visible in the dark when the headlights of a car hit the reflective surface.

In Finland it's the law to wear a reflector when it's dark. As countries with mandatory or prevalent reflector use have the lowest rates of pedestrian accidents per capita, it seems like a simple and sensible solution for traffic safety. Especially compared to the more complicated measures in other parts of the world to address pedestrian visibility such as suggesting people carry flashlights, not wear black or don reflective tape.

Considered consumption

Design thinking touches just about every area of life in Finland, including the vibrant second-hand scene that addresses a range of issues from community spirit to sustainable consumption to the sharing economy.

One very good example of this is Cleaning Day.

Twice a year throughout the country, city parks, sidewalks and inner courtyards are transformed into a massive public outdoor flea market. Vendors are regular folks, who at no cost can set up shop for the day to flog their wares, ranging from pre-owned clothing and accessories to dishes and flatware, toys, books and whatever else they want to sell.

The celebration of recycling and positive community spirit takes place each May and August. It's based on the simple idea that people clean out their cupboards, closets, and attics of unwanted or unused items for a day (or two, rather) and sell them to others.

Like many locals and families with children, I use the event as a way to look for specific items. As children grow quickly out of clothing and toys, there's little point in spending large sums of money on something that you can pick up in near to mint condition for a fraction of the cost. Second-hand shopping can be much more sustainable and practical than purchasing something new.

At Cleaning Days over the years, I've picked up a range of items: an iconic Marimekko red-striped T-shirt for my son for far less than it would have cost in the shops; a pair of never-worn blue rubber rain boots for him to splash about in puddles; toy cars, trains and Lego; and sturdy design classics such as Iittala water glasses – a steal at a few euros a piece – that will likely stand the test of time as well as retain their value.

Not only is this type of shopping easy on my budget, it's a fun way to spend a few hours with my son outdoors stopping in public parks where there's a concentration of sellers and the possibility of seeing friends. It's also a way to teach my son that in a world where there's already too much stuff it's a good idea to consider looking for pre-owned items before buying brand-new ones.

One worrying fact is that of the 80 billion pieces of clothing produced worldwide annually, only a quarter will be recycled – the rest go to landfills or are incinerated, according to Greenpeace in 2016.

Intrigued by the idea of Cleaning Day, I chat with Jaakko Blomberg, the Helsinki Sauna Day founder, as he's also been involved in organising Cleaning Day.

The event works on several levels that go far beyond the concept of the flea market.

Blomberg says that in addition to the message about considered consumption – buy-it-used-rather-than-new – there are other important messages to be gleaned. One is that well-made, long-lasting, durable items, such as Nordic design classics, are a better investment than fast fashion.

Considered consumption – buy it used rather than new

'Although there's a general eco-awareness in the air on Cleaning Day, we want people to wake up to the fact that cheap, poor-quality clothing that's unethically produced doesn't get sold,' he says. 'If you have good-quality items, they last and there's always an interested buyer. This is something very important that we want to communicate – less stuff, more quality items that are ethically produced.

'I once heard a seventy-year-old woman saying, "I'll never buy anything new again because I can buy everything from Cleaning Day and flea markets." I do think it's helped to change consumer behaviour,' Blomberg continues.

'Many people have told me that they've started to expand the idea to other areas of consumption; they're thinking: "Do I really need this thing?"'

~~~

The idea for Cleaning Day originated with Pauliina Seppälä, who has been a key force behind many Finnish platforms and events that bring people and ideas with a positive common cause related to sharing and sustainability together using social media.

Seppälä is a producer and co-founder of Yhteismaa ('Common Ground') a non-profit organisation that specialises in participatory city culture, inclusiveness and social movements.

As I want to find out more about the roots of this community spirit that celebrates the sharing economy, I get in touch with her.

She is sporting jeans and colourful sneakers when I meet her near a square overlooking the building site of Oodi, the new 98-million-euro Helsinki central library, which will of course have a sauna, that's due to open in 2018.

Our venue seems fitting, as libraries are an excellent example of the sharing economy. Finns are the world's leading book borrowers, with 67 million books borrowed a year from the public library system. The system offers a range of free services that extend to borrowing board games and movies, offering computer and scanner access, and in some locations the possibility to use equipment such as sewing machines or a 3D-printer, and of course a place to study or work.

When I ask Seppälä where the idea for Cleaning Day originated, she says that the seeds were planted when she was living in Amsterdam with her family many years ago.

'Every Sunday was garbage day and people could leave unwanted items on the kerb for others to take. We had an empty flat when we arrived. On the street there was all sorts of stuff, including furniture that we picked up because we needed a couch,' she says.

Back in Helsinki over dinner with friends one evening, a discussion arose about how to facilitate a similar type of event. Later, when a Cleaning Day Facebook group was started, it had close to 6,000 members within twenty-four hours.

'That fascinated me, as it illustrated the power of social media,' says Seppälä. She credits the Cleaning Day concept catching on so quickly to its successful predecessor Restaurant Day, a day when anyone can be a restaurateur by pitching up a kiosk or mini-restaurant; the idea has spread to more than seventy-five countries since its inception in Finland in 2011.

Cleaning Day's social media site has become an ecological-lifestyle information channel, with people sharing information about everything from recycling to greenwashing.

'It was great to see how something that started with zero budget really activated people and flourished into something much greater,' says Seppälä.

I ask her where this down-to-earth approach that's not focused on making a profit comes from. Is it rooted in Finland's difficult past – in the last hundred years Finland has gone from being one of the world's poorest countries to one of the wealthiest – a frugal attitude, or a type of *sisu*?

'We have this morality, which has its roots in a Protestant ethic that waste is wrong, we value neither waste nor vanity,' she replies.

An anti-materialistic philosophy is something that Blomberg also commented on when I asked him about it: 'You don't need to boost your ego or your position in society through material possessions – showing off has never been the done thing here.'

Both Blomberg and Seppälä stress that Cleaning Day, like so many community initiatives they've been involved with, have been created by the people. Yhteismaa initially produced the design-thinking framework and then it was the general public, together with the help of technology, who took it from there using tools such as Google Maps.

The small-is-beautiful community ethic runs through many areas of life, accompanied by the refreshing notion that you don't need a lot of money to make a difference.

Seppälä has also set up many community platforms that aim to help others, including the Refugee Hospitality Club, which connects those who want to offer support in the wake of the European migrant crisis that started in 2015, for example by volunteering their time or donating much-needed items at reception centres in Finland.

The small-is-beautiful community ethic runs through many areas of life, accompanied by the refreshing notion that you don't need a lot of money to make a difference.

'The Refugee Hospitality Club really woke me up to the power of social media, a small budget, and what you can do – throw the idea out there and the collective intelligence and creativity of the group is much much greater,' says Seppälä.

Another of Seppälä's team's initiatives is the Nappi Naapuri neighbour network, based on the idea that everyone registered in the online service has the opportunity to help others nearby with the push of a button. For example, someone has a sick child and urgently needs a packet of diapers from the shop but can't leave the child alone. It may be easy for a neighbour to pick up a packet while they do their own shopping and drop it off.

Seppälä also provides another example, which is fitting for a world with an ageing population: 'I could easily go and help a senior with a small task when I'm on my way to work. Care costs for the elderly are constantly increasing, so in addition to a personal caregiver, you could have a helping neighbour to fill some gaps. The service economy is based on people's know-how, and often that know-how means simply having a pair of helping hands,' she says.

People come together without commercial gain in mind, but rather for the common good of everyone.

'Part of the thinking behind equality is the idea that everything doesn't have to be commercial. Many things can be high quality and open for everyone – such as healthcare and education – and it's not always necessary to find the best business model that makes the most money. Sometimes a good business model is enough,' says Seppälä.

This way of thinking strikes me as a modern version of the Finnish *talkoot* tradition – a communal work concept based on everyone pitching in, whether it's volunteers helping to clean or maintain national parks, or all the residents of an apartment block or housing complex spending an afternoon raking the leaves or taking care of other yard work together.

Less is more

A recent bestseller on the topic of less is more, James Wallman's excellent *Stuffocation: Living More with Less* strikes a particular chord with me. In his well-written book, trend forecaster Wallman illustrates several key concepts, including how shifting the focus from possessions to experiences and away from consumption can actually make people happier and healthier.

Movements such as the tiny house movement and voluntary simplicity embrace the idea that having less stuff and living smaller can have a range of benefits, including less debt, which can increase wellbeing by reducing stress and freeing up time.

One of the marked differences that I notice early on in my Nordic immersion is that Finns, and many European city dwellers for that matter, tend to live in much smaller spaces than North Americans.

I'm generalising, of course, because there are Finns and Europeans who live in big houses and North Americans who live in small apartments. But whereas many of my friends in North American cities tend to move out to houses in the suburbs when they have children, the reverse seems to be the case here.

We live in a two-bedroom apartment that is centrally located in Helsinki and within a bike ride, walk or tram from just about everywhere that we need to go. The idea of moving further out of the city just to have more space and more stuff (and a longer commute that might not be bikeable) holds little appeal. I no longer harbour the dream of a house with a garden, as I once did. Perhaps because we spend a lot of time outdoors there's less need for so much of our own space; we have so much shared community space. Instead of aspiring to a bigger or better apartment, I feel a sense of gratitude for what I have. This is a change from the attitude I had during my formative years when I spent a lot of time yearning for things I didn't have.

But it takes me several years of living in northern Europe to arrive at my small-is-Zen attitude. Of course, it helps that many of my friends in cities such as London tend to live in compact apartments rather than houses. And because so many people that I know here live the same way.

According to the Finnish Environment Institute (SYKE), and their 2016 Resident Survey, which surveys the quality of urban residential environments and aspirations: 'the greatest change in aspirations of where to live and in lifestyles has occurred in thirty- to forty-year-olds and in families with children whose aspirations for city centre living and living in blocks of flats have increased the most. The advantage of city centres is the functional variety; they combine living, work, services, leisure opportunities and the availability of culture as well as good transport connections.'

But it is my shift in appreciation to what James Wallman and many others have described, away from possessions and towards experiences, that clinches it.

For example, cycling everywhere is something that makes me happy. I wouldn't want to give that up just to live in a bigger space with more things.

The pared-down Nordic lifestyle helps me to appreciate the functional and practical.

Perhaps I no longer feel that I need to keep up with the Joneses because I live in a relatively egalitarian society where the differences between rich and poor, though admittedly growing, are not so great.

Katja Pantzar

Pre-loved charm

I have always appreciated a second-hand score and on my travels have sought out thrift shops and flea markets from New York to Berlin.

But here it feels like a lifestyle, as so many people shop this way. On reflection, I think it's part of the strong eco-awareness that I've picked up while living here. But it's also personal. As I swim in the sea daily, I have a vested interest in keeping the water clean, whether that's by avoiding buying water in plastic bottles whenever possible or considering the long-term effects of my consumption habits.

In keeping with the Cleaning Day sustainability philosophy, along with keeping an eye on my budget, I use the city's numerous self-service flea markets and online marketplaces to first search for specific items before heading to a department store or high-street shop.

I've furnished much of my apartment this way, from a kitchen table and chairs to a nearly-new designer sofa that would have originally cost four times what I paid for it.

I am so happy with our pre-loved couch that I never look at it and wish I could have bought a new one. It makes sense on so many levels; I don't even have to worry about the 'new couch' when my son and his friends are playing on it.

~~~~~~~

It's likely owing to the strong culture of trust that exists here – if you say you're going to do something, you do it, which I've come to view as a *sisu* quality similar to not quitting – that I've had mainly positive experiences shopping second-hand. To this day I've never been cheated on an item that I've bought at a flea market or through an online marketplace. The product descriptions have always been more or less accurate, transactions straightforward, and sellers have always delivered an item at the agreed-upon time.

This culture of trust and honesty is highly regarded here.

Internationally, one of the commonly referenced honesty surveys is the 2013 *Reader's Digest* wallet test. Helsinki was found to be the most honest city in the world in a test where wallets were 'dropped' in sixteen major cities by the magazine. In the Finnish capital, eleven out of twelve wallets dropped by the magazine were returned.

Katja Pantzar

Creating a functional lifestyle

My Nordic design immersion also teaches me to apply design thinking to other areas of my life.

In addition to creating a functional lifestyle in areas of wellbeing such as winter swimming and cycling all year round, I tap into a kind of *sisu* self-discipline, which means that I make an effort to organise my working life in a healthy way as well.

As I've been self-employed for the past five years, I work off the grid, so to speak. My schedule varies greatly from day to day. As a fairly social person, I'm happy to spend several days a month in a newsroom surrounded by people or in-house at a publishing firm editing a magazine.

But the nature of being a freelance writer means that I often spend a lot of time on my own. Because working alone can leave me feeling isolated, I've found that renting a desk in a shared workspace makes a huge difference to my mood, as I'm surrounded by like-minded souls such as other freelance writers and journalists.

Not only is it healthy to take a proper lunch break at a nearby restaurant with these people, I also benefit from being able to get advice and support (and sometimes a shoulder to cry on) from others who do the same type of work as I do.

And I intentionally chose a space that's not far from home, but not too close because it means that on the days I go to the workspace, I get in a five-kilometre round-trip by bicycle. My short ride that winds along the shoreline is faster than any other form of transport. The distance is also walkable.

Serendipitously, our modest workspace lies just down the hill from a church whose bells chime a melody composed by Sibelius twice a day. Every time they sound, I'm reminded of the famous composer's take on that special Finnish fortitude: '*Sisu* is like a metaphorical shot in the arm that allows the individual to do what's impossible.'

Creating a simpler and more sustainable lifestyle

- *Consider your consumption – where will this item go when I'm done with it? Can it be donated or re-sold?*
- *Is buying second-hand an option?*
- *Invest in a few well-made items that will last longer than many poor-quality ones that will likely end up in the garbage.*
- *Tap into sisu and make the effort to design a more functional lifestyle where possible: would less stuff or a smaller living space address quality-of-life issues such as reducing your budget or maintenance costs or your daily commute?*

Conclusion: finding your *sisu*

~~~~~~~~

One of my great inspirations and joys in life is my son. Over the years, as he has grown from a baby into a boy, I have watched as he has learned a range of skills from walking and talking, reading and writing, to swimming and riding a bicycle. Every step of the way, his fierce determination to master each new skill has greatly impressed and intrigued me. What is that quality that sees him fall off his bike, kick the tyres in frustration, and then dust himself off and climb back into the saddle to give it another try?

That quality is, of course, *sisu*.

His attitude of not giving up inspires me to be stronger and more resilient, to not bow out when I feel frustrated or tired. Watching him reinforces all that I have learned along my journey in Finland about drawing on my own *sisu*.

In these pages I have approached the Finnish lifestyle in much the same way that a travel writer might capture a new destination: by observing, researching and writing about the positive elements that are worth putting into print. Which practices, customs and habits foster wellbeing? Which ones are worth exploring and sharing with others? Central to many of these practices is this special Finnish fortitude.

If you were to ask me now how I would define *sisu*, I would reply that it's a courageous mindset that embraces challenges, both small and big; it's the ability to act in the face of adversity; it's an approach to life that is open to trying new things, experiences and going beyond what we think our limits might be – whether physical, mental or emotional; it's also about looking for practical solutions and ways to move forward, to build up fortitude and resilience.

Finding *sisu*, as I have tried to illustrate here, allows for simple and sensible lifestyle solutions that boost wellbeing, from nature therapy to the Nordic diet. Exercising daily *sisu* means implementing self-care by doing simple things such as getting fresh air and exercise, eating a well-balanced diet and making time for enough rest. A strong body builds a strong mind. I very much agree with what my fellow winter swimmer Douglas said: 'Sisu requires a positive exercise of will, it's a muscle you exercise.'

Regardless of where we live and what we do, we all struggle with so many of the same issues in our daily lives. And in finding a sense of our *sisu* by taking care of our wellbeing, we become stronger, more balanced, and better able to address universal health concerns and stresses.

On a practical level, that might be as simple as taking small steps towards building a functional lifestyle that incorporates incidental exercise, walking or cycling to work perhaps, or trying activities such as cold-water swimming or going for a stroll in nature. I learned first-hand through practices such as winter swimming just how my own fortitude, my own sense of *sisu*, could be harnessed, and used to help me consider what else I might be capable of.

Though the roots of *sisu* lie in a type of icy Nordic practicality and determination, anyone, anywhere, can tap into their own form of it. That might mean not always choosing the easy way – for example, house cleaning or raking leaves rather than outsourcing those tasks. Maintaining a connection to nature in daily life, whether by heading to a beach or forest for a walk, or making time for a stroll in the park, is equally important.

In an unstable world where there are so many issues to be concerned about, from climate change to political and financial instability, tapping into a *sisu* mindset can offer a way forward, finding and building on your inner strength and resilience to help you deal with life's challenges.

Good *sisu* management also means that when something is troubling me, instead of keeping it to myself I make the effort to talk to a friend. I know that as soon as I say the words out loud, part of the problem will diminish just by the act of sharing it. And more often than not, when I ask for help, I find a simple solution that I might not have thought of on my own.

When faced with a challenge, even if I feel anxious or nervous, I tell myself to gather up my *sisu*, and figure out what I need to do next, who I may need to ask for help and how best to take on the challenge.

One of the key things I've learned about finding my *sisu* is that you don't need to set huge goals. You don't need to win Olympic medals. It can start with very small steps that you can implement right now that can lead to larger changes. If I can do it, so can you.

Here's an example of a simple *sisu*-filled day:

Consider setting your alarm in the morning for thirty minutes earlier than your usual time and instead of hitting the snooze button, summon up your *sisu* and get yourself out of bed and into your gym gear and out the door. Even an energising early morning walk can do wonders for mind and body. Take time to notice your surroundings. If there's nature nearby, focus on the trees, grass, plants, nearby water or the sky.

When you return home, make yourself a healthy and nourishing breakfast in order to fuel your body so that you're not running on an empty tank. You can test your *sisu* throughout the day by summoning up the courage to have that difficult conversation with your colleague, friend or neighbour. Or start that work project that you've been putting off. Ensure that you eat a healthy and balanced meal for lunch. In the evening, on the way home, get off the train, tube or bus one or two stops before your destination and walk the rest of the way to get some incidental exercise. Approach house cleaning as incidental exercise and DIY *sisu*. Exercise your *sisu* by sticking with a book or language course or mending project that you've been putting off. Consider taking on whatever daily challenges, small or big, suit you best.

When it comes to tackling bigger challenges, one of the phrases that has stayed with me is *sisu* expert Emilia Lahti's line about mindset: '*Sisu* gives rise to what I call an action mindset; a courageous attitude which contributes to how we approach challenges. *Sisu* is a way of life to actively transform the challenges that come our way into opportunities.' Without an action mindset, if you don't believe you can run a marathon you're unlikely to take the first steps to do so. Now this doesn't mean that you need to run a marathon, but the idea is to bring an open mind to trying new things and start taking action, even if they're small steps, towards those goals.

Anyone anywhere could use a little *sisu* or fortitude in their daily lives to feel healthier and ultimately happier. It's really about moving outside of your comfort zone in a positive way – can you challenge yourself to take healthy risks, try new experiences, and consider going beyond your limits, whether physical, mental or emotional?

Perhaps the most important aspect of healthy *sisu* is finding what works for you. Winter swimming and year-round cycling may not be for everyone. This is one of the key *sisu* takeaways: that special spirit of resilience honours independence and autonomy; it's about being your own *sisu* scriptwriter.

Epilogue

When I think back to those three young men running down that snowy Helsinki street towards the dock in their bathrobes and slippers, I feel a sense of gratitude. For like my friends Tiina and Riikka, who introduced me to the icy waters of the Baltic Sea, they started me on a journey.

Though I have discovered many sources of strength, courage and joy from the pared-down Nordic lifestyle, it was largely through the art of winter swimming that I learned how to tap into that special Finnish quality of resilience, *sisu*. Not only did I find a natural and effective method for dealing with a range of ailments; the practice also led to an exploration of other ways, such as forest therapy, to boost a sense of wellbeing.

Though some might hold that *sisu* is a cultural

characteristic, I think it's an approach, an attitude towards life of not giving up and, of challenging yourself, which can be learned. If I have learned to flex my *sisu* muscle, anyone can. And it doesn't always need to be extreme. Sometimes the smallest changes can lead to bigger ones. As *sisu* expert Emilia Lahti so eloquently put it: 'If you don't believe you can do something, you won't take the steps to do it.'

For my part, I started to question my belief that I couldn't do certain things because I suffered from depression and anxiety. I started taking steps towards change because I realised that even small steps could lead to bigger ones. One of those steps is telling my story – which is perhaps my biggest act of *sisu* to date – in the hopes that it can help others, instead of them hiding behind a façade of trying to pretend that everything is fine, something I've managed to do well for many years. People are often quite surprised to find out that I suffer from depression, as they say I come across as an optimistic person. But by accepting what I perceive to be one of my weaknesses, I have found strength through talking openly about my struggles. Though I am in a good place now, I know that I need to take care of myself physically and mentally in order to stay there and keep the symptoms of depression at bay.

In the interests of disclosure, as I was finishing this manuscript, some major life changes took place on the home front. My husband and I made the incredibly difficult decision to divorce. Our lifestyles had just become very different over the years. It is too raw and too soon to reflect properly, or write anything of significance about this. But it is fair to say the decision was made together, diplomatically and with our son's best interests at heart.

And perhaps this is one of the greatest lessons that I have learned about *sisu*.

As one wise British editor said: '*Sisu* is about getting comfortable with discomfort.' It's about recognising and acknowledging when a change might be necessary, such as in an unhappy relationship, no matter how difficult it may be. And having the courage to let go.

In the interests of fairness, I should also point out there was nothing to stop me adopting these elements of the Nordic lifestyle in the other cities where I've lived – London, Vancouver and Toronto all have a range of fabulous outdoor and wellness opportunities. But for me, it wasn't until I moved north that I really learned how to simplify my lifestyle and shift my focus from weakness to strength and find my own sense of *sisu*.

For me, that made all the difference in the world.

Sisu

- *Pronounced 'see-su'.*
- *A unique type of Finnish fortitude, of not giving up in the face of a challenge, big or small, that anyone can develop.*
- *An attitude of turning challenges into opportunities.*
- *An ancient Finnish concept that dates back to the 1500s.*

Appendices

~

Winter swimming tips

If you want to try winter swimming, a good tip is to gradually acclimatise your body by continuing to swim when summer ends. This helps your body to adjust to gradually colder water temperatures.

First ensure that you're in good health and fit to try winter swimming.

General guidelines and common sense hold that if you're sick you should not go into the water, nor should you go if you suffer from illness such as a heart condition, high blood pressure, asthma or other medical conditions without first consulting a doctor.

When the winter swimming season starts, go with a friend who is an experienced winter swimmer and has access to a winter swimming spot.

If you don't have neoprene slippers, you can wear wool socks or flip-flops as you walk to the water.

For the first time, let it simply be a dip. If you can't go all the way into the water, that's fine. Try to remember to breathe.

If there's a sauna option in conjunction with winter swimming that can make it much easier mentally and physically – being able to warm up afterwards can make the icy prospect much less daunting.

After warming up in a sauna, you may find yourself wanting to try it again because it feels so good.

Remember to stay hydrated by drinking water.

Practical cycling tips

I cycle all year round, no matter what the weather. I live in a climate where temperatures can range from minus 20 degrees Celsius to 30 degrees Celsius, which requires a practical and flexible wardrobe.

As I don't need to wear suits or pencil skirts or heels for work, I can dress quite casually.

For the summer months, I've created a wardrobe that's cycle-friendly and includes plenty of skirts and dresses. My criteria for purchasing a skirt or dress: does it flare from the waist or is it made of stretchy fabric? I can pair those up with thin cycling shorts that are not bulky or visible but that are invaluable if my skirt does fly up while I'm pedalling.

I carry a small freshening-up kit with me. If I'm biking longer distances and need to arrive at an important meeting looking fresh, I pack a travel kit with soap and moisturiser, a comb, and toothbrush and toothpaste along with a small hand towel. I find a large towel is unnecessary and adds too much bulk and weight to my bag. I use the ladies room to freshen up with a bit of soap and water, for example to wash my face.

If I know there will be showering facilities, I include shower travel-size bottles of shampoo and conditioner. Most workplaces that have shower facilities in Finland also have a communal hairdryer.

As for the winter, one of the beauties of biking during the cooler months is that it's less of a sweat.

During the dark months, I ensure that my bike has plenty of lights and I wear several reflectors. I even have a somewhat stylish black vest with white reflector stripes instead of a yellow one to lessen the construction worker look.

During the winter months I use winter tyres with spikes. I find they often provide more stability than walking when snow has melted and frozen and created a temporary skating rink in parts of the city.

A set of durable rain proofs is an excellent investment, as clothes stay clean and dry whatever the weather.

For very cold weather it's essential to have a warm hat, gloves and wool socks. For even colder temperatures, a face mask made of a cotton-silk blend with an opening for the eyes and nose that's easy to breathe through but keeps you warm – or a lined woollen one also does the trick – is invaluable.

Winter cycling, like many other cold-weather activities, is only cold for the first couple of minutes; then, as you start moving, your body warms up.

Some cyclists carry a change of clothes in their panniers. It's really about what works best for you and your lifestyle.

How to sauna Finnish style

The sauna is a sacred place for many Finns. It's a place to relax and cleanse both mind and body.

Shower before and after taking a sauna.

There are no rules about how long to sit in the sauna. It's completely up to you. After a few minutes, the hot steam, which can be between 70 and 100 degrees Celsius, will relax muscles.

As for the *löyly*, the water that's ladled onto the sauna stove's hot rocks to create steam and increase heat, courtesy holds that you don't throw *löyly* without first asking others in the sauna if it's alright.

Sauna-goers often take with them what's known as a *pefletti*, a seat cover made of linen, terrycloth or a sheet of thick paper (these are often on offer in public saunas), for hygiene reasons.

In a women-only or a men-only sauna, the usual practice is to be naked. In mixed saunas, those for both men and women, swimsuits are worn.

Though there are no hard and fast rules about topics of discussion in the sauna — they vary depending on the place and the group of people assembled – as it's a place for relaxing, the atmosphere should be respectful of others.

The main goal is to enjoy the experience.

Acknowledgements

I am full of gratitude to the many inspiring people – and work assignments – that took me to the waters, woods, saunas and other inspiring places of Finland.

I owe a huge thank you to the dozens of people I interviewed for this book who graciously gave me their time and generously shared their stories, thoughts and ideas: Tiina Torppa, who I met shortly after I arrived in Finland is a wonderful friend and a role model of a strong, independent woman who juggles family and a successful career with a myriad of other talents; Riikka Toivanen, who first took me winter swimming; inspiring *sisu* expert Emilia Lahti; and lovely cold expert Professor Hannu Rintamäki. I could go on at length about all of my interviewees, who have been amazing and inspiring each in their own way. Thank you

Katja Pantzar

Patrik Borg, Pauliina Seppälä, Pasi Sahlberg, Jaakko Blomberg, Niklas Aalto-Setälä, Liisa Tyrväinen, Timo Perälä, Seppo Uski, Sanna Jahkola, Barbara Schneider, Ilkka Vuori, André Noël Chaker, Timo Nuuminen, Pia Lipponen, S. Douglas Olson, Päivi Pälvimäki and Veikko Tuovinen. And thank you to the many people who helped me to verify facts or point me in the right direction, including Taru Laanti, Timo Partonen, Paula Paronen, Pirkko Huttunen and Birgitta Järvinen.

I'm not sure that this book would exist yet without my agents Elina Ahlbäck, Eleonoora Kirk and Lotta Dufva, who championed it when it was merely a proposal, a few sample chapters and an outline. Thank you! Although I've had the idea for the book since 2010, a special expression of gratitude goes to Elina, who reached out to me, encouraged me, and facilitated the writing process by securing advances that allowed me to write full-time for several months.

And a big thank you to Hannah Black, my first editor and publisher, who also championed this idea before it was a book and made excellent editorial suggestions and guided me through the editorial process with her wonderful team at Hodder, including editorial assistant Ian Wong and copyeditor Sophie Elletson.

Thank you also to all the other editors and publishers and publicists who got on board when this book was just a proposal and a few sample chapters: WUJ (Poland), Yeeyan Publishing (China), Belfond (France), Mladá Fronta (Czech Republic), Bastei Lübbe (Germany), Marsilio/ Sonzogno (Italy), Kosmos (Netherlands), AST (Russia), Roca Editorial (Spain) and TarcherPerigee/Penguin Random House (US).

And thanks to my early readers who provided invaluable feedback and support: Elina Ahlbäck, Lotta Dufva, Eleonoora Kirk, Tiina Torppa, Anu Silfverberg, Satu Pantzar, Tapio Pantzar, Senja Larsen, Susan Huotari, and to Riina Tamm, who kindly read and edited a very early version of the first few chapters and proposal and made great suggestions back in 2014.

I am very grateful for my supportive family and friends: my parents Satu and Tapio; my son Felix, who lights up my life every day; to Harpal and Tino; Sammy, Susan, Andreas, Connie, Riina, Tracey and all those who have cheered me on at work and play, including Soili, Denise, Aleksi, Amanda and Egan.

And thanks to the Kallio workspace gang: Hanna, Anu, Jussi, Juha, Esa, Antti, Sanna, Mirja and Suvi, who listened to me, supported me and inspired me through the thick and thin of the writing process, and to Jussi for lending me his chair, which made all the difference.

And I also owe a big thank you to all of my fellow cold-water and winter swimmers, who, along with the transformative qualities of the water, make each day just a little bit better and brighter.

References

Active Healthy Kids Canada 2014 Report Card on Physical Activity for Children and Youth, *Is Canada in the Running?: How Canada Stacks Up Against 14 Other Countries on Physical Activity for Children and Youth*, Toronto, Canada: Active Healthy Kids.

Anthes, Emily (12 May 2016), 'The Glossary of Happiness', *The New Yorker*, New York, NY: Condé Nast.

Bains, Camille (14 June 2017), 'Canada ranked 25th on children's wellbeing amongst rich countries: UNICEF', *Globe and Mail*, Toronto, Canada.

Beres, Damon (September 2013), 'Most Honest Cities: The *Reader's Digest* Lost Wallet Test', *Reader's Digest*, New York, NY: Trusted Media Brands.

Berkeley Wellness (12 June 2014), 'The New Nordic Diet', University of California Berkeley, San Francisco: Berkeley Wellness.

Borg, Patrik (2009), *Syö hyvin ja laihdu*, Helsinki, Finland: Otava Publishing.

Chaker, André Noël (2017), *The Finnish Miracle: 100 Years of Success*, Helsinki, Finland: Alma Talent.

Corliss, Julie (19 November 2015), 'The Nordic diet: Healthy eating with an eco-friendly bent', *Harvard Heart Letter*, Boston, Massachusetts: Harvard Medical School.

Cuthbertson, Anthony (24 February 2017), 'The Cold Sell: Why Tech Startups are Pitching from an Ice Hole in Finland', *Newsweek*, New York, NY: IBT Media

Dovey, Ceridwen (9 June 2015), 'Can Reading Make You Happier?', *The New Yorker*.

Duckworth, Angela (2016), *Grit: The Power of Passion and Perseverance*, New York, NY: Scribner.

Economist Intelligence Unit (2012), 'Starting well: Benchmarking early education across the world', London, England: Economist Group.

'Finnish recommendations for physical activity in early childhood 2016: Joy, play and doing together' (2016:35), Helsinki, Finland: Ministry of Education and Culture.

Foroohar, Rana (16 August 2010), 'The Best Countries in the World', *Newsweek*, New York, NY: IBT Media.

Gill, Jason and Cellis-Morales, Carlos (20 April 2017), 'Cycling to work: major new study suggests health benefits are staggering' *The Conversation*, UK edition, London: The Conversation Trust.

Goodrich, Austin (1960), *Study in Sisu: Finland's Fight for Independence*, New York, NY: Ballantine Books.

Harper, Mark (20 December 2016), 'Fewer illnesses, less stress: How cold-water swimming can change your life', *Spectator Health*, London, England: Press Holdings.

Harvard Health Publishing (March 2014), 'Sauna Health Benefits: Are saunas healthy or harmful?', Boston, Massachusetts: Harvard Medical School.

Heikura Pasi, Huttunen Pirkko and Kinnunen, Taina (2000), *Hyinen Hurmio: Avantouimarin käsikirja*, Helsinki, Finland: Edita Publishing.

Helliwell, J., Layard, R., and Sachs, J. (2017), 'World Happiness Report 2017', New York: Sustainable Development Solutions Network.

Howlett, Karen and Weeks, Carly (18 August 2015), 'Prescriptions of opioid drugs skyrocketing in Canada', *Globe and Mail*, Toronto, Canada.

Howlett, Karen (27 March 2017), 'Prescriptions for painkillers still rising in Canada despite opioid crisis', *Globe and Mail*, Toronto, Canada.

Huttunen, Pirkko *et al.* (2004), 'Winter swimming improves general well-being', *International Journal of Circumpolar Health*, Co-Action Publishing on behalf of the Circumpolar Health Research Network.

Hämäläinen, Timo J. and Michaelson, Juliet (2014), *Well-being and Beyond: Broadening the Policy Discourse*, Cheltenham, UK: Edward Elgar Publishing Limited/Sitra, the Finnish Innovation Fund.

James, Sandy (13 January 2017), 'Opinion: Visibility plays major role in pedestrian deaths', *Vancouver Sun*, Vancouver, Canada: Postmedia Network Inc.

Jansson, Tove (2003), *The Summer Book* (translated by Thomas Teal), London, UK: Sort of Books.

Jansson, Tove (2006), *The Winter Book* (translated by Silvester Mazzarella, David McDuff and Kingsley Hart), London, UK: Sort of Books.

Järnefelt, Heli (2016), 'Työikäisten hyvän unen avaimet', Terveysliikuntauutiset 2016, Tampere, Finland: UKK Institute.

Kallio, Veikko (1989), *Finland: Cultural Perspectives*, Helsinki, Finland: WSOY.

Kallionpää, Katri (1 October 2016), 'Sauna tekee sydämelle hyvää – tämä ja neljä muuta syytä mennä viikonloppuna saunaan', *Helsingin Sanomat,* Helsinki, Finland: Sanoma Media Finland.

Kallunki, Elisa (4 May 2017), 'Tutkimukset todistavat, että metsä on mahtava stressilääke: Laskee sydämen sykettä ja vähentää lihasjännitystä', Helsinki, Finland: Yle Uutiset.

Khazan, Olga (11 July 2013), 'The Secret to Finland's Success with Schools, Moms, Kids – and Everything', *The Atlantic,* Washington, DC: Atlantic Media.

Koay, Jacqueline (18 April 2017), 'From Finland, Teach Children *Sisu*', The Blog, Huffington Post UK.

Koskela, Elina (21 September 2013), 'Luonto hoitaa ja metsä parantaa', *Ilkka,* Seinäjoki, Finland: I-Mediat Oy.

Kujanpää, Risto and Helsinki City Planning Department (2015), 'Helsinki Bicycle Account 2015', Helsinki, Finland: Helsinki City Planning Department.

Lahti, Emilia (15 December 2014), 'Sisu – transforming barriers into frontiers', TEDxTurku, YouTube, http://www.youtube.com/watch?v=UTlieGyf5kU, accessed December 2017.

Landreth, Jenny (13 February 2017), 'Brrr! The Joys of Cold Water Swimming', *Telegraph,* London, England: Telegraph Media Group.

Laukkanen, Tanjaniina, Kunutsor, Setor, Kauhanen, Jussi, Laukkanen, Jari (7 December 2016), 'Sauna bathing is inversely associated with dementia and Alzheimer's disease in middle-aged Finnish men', *Age and Ageing*, Oxford University Press, Oxford, UK.

Lee, Helena (14 June 2013), 'Why Finnish babies sleep in cardboard boxes', BBC News magazine, London, UK: BBC.

Lehmuskoski, Susanna (18 June 2017), 'Vähemmän kaikkea, parempi elämä', *Helsingin Sanomat*, Helsinki, Finland: Sanoma Media Finland.

Luckhurst, Phoebe (12 December 2016), 'Forget Denmark and *hygge*, Finland is the new Nordic hotspot for wellbeing', *Evening Standard*, London, England: Associated Newspapers.

Malmberg, Katarina (16 April 2017), 'Metsässä treeni tuntuu kevyeltä ja juoksu muuttuu rennoksi – Kokeile viittä terveyttä lisäävää luontoliikuntalajia', *Helsingin Sanomat*, Helsinki, Finland: Sanoma Media Finland.

Mogensen, Klaus Æ. (02/2013), 'The Bicycle – The Future Means of Transportation', *Scenario Magazine*, Copenhagen, Denmark: Copenhagen Institute for Futures Studies.

'Northern Theatre: *Sisu*' (8 January 1940), *Time*, New York, NY: Time Warner.

Oaklander, Mandy (18 April 2016), 'How to Eat Like a Nordic Person', *Time Health,* New York, NY: Time Warner.

Partanen, Anu (2016), *The Nordic Theory of Everything: In Search of a Better Life,* New York, NY: HarperCollins Publishers.

Partanen, Anu (11 December 2011), 'What Americans Keep Ignoring About Finland's School Success', *The Atlantic,* Washington, DC: Atlantic Media.

Porter, Michael E., Stern, Scott and Green, Michael (2016), 'Social Progress Index 2016: Executive Summary', Social Progress Index.

Puttonen, Mikko (29 September 2017), 'Saunominen laskee verenpainetta, osoittavat suomalaisväestöllä tehdyt tutkimukset – mutta saunassa on käytävä tietyin väliajoin', *Helsingin Sanomat,* Helsinki, Finland: Sanoma Media Finland.

Pölkki, Minna (3 September 2014), 'Suomen hiljaisuutta markkinoidaan Aasiaan', *Helsingin Sanomat,* Helsinki, Finland: Sanoma Media Finland.

Rautava, Timo (13 October 2008), 'Venyttele haravan kanssa', *Helsingin Sanomat,* Helsinki, Finland: Sanoma Media Finland.

Repo, Päivi (23 July 2017), 'Lihavuus lisääntyy joka puolella maailmaa – Suomessa on lihavia Ruotsia enemmän,

mutta maailmassa olemme vain keskitasoa, kertoo 195
maan vertailu', *Helsingin Sanomat,* Helsinki, Finland:
Sanoma Media Finland.

Ruusunen, Anu (2013), 'Diet and depression: An
epidemiological study', University of Eastern Finland,
Faculty of Health Sciences, Publications of the University
of Eastern Finland, Dissertations in Health Sciences 185.

Sahlberg, Pasi (2015), *Finnish Lessons 2.0: What Can the
World Learn from Educational Change in Finland?,* 2nd
edition, New York, NY: Teachers College Press.

Sander, Gordon F. (2013), *The Hundred-Day Winter War:
Finland's Gallant Stand Against the Soviet Army,*
Lawrence, Kansas: University Press of Kansas.

Seminar: Liikunta lääkkeenä – työikäiset liikunnan monikäyttäjiksi
(11–12 October 2016), the UKK Institute, Helsinki, Finland.

Shakersain, Behnaz *et al.* (13 September 2015), 'Healthy
Diet May Reduce Cognitive Decline As People Age',
Karolinska Institutet

Shevchuk, Nikolai A. (2008), 'Adapted cold shower as a
potential treatment for depression', *Medical
Hypotheses,* Amsterdam, The Netherlands.

Sillanpää, Anna (15 September 2014), 'Näin metsä hoitaa
mieltäsi', *Kodin Kuvalehti,* Sanoma Magazines, Helsinki,
Finland: Sanoma Media Finland.

Seminar on SISU, (8 May 2017), Finnish Academy of Science and Letters, Helsinki, Finland.

Strandell, Anna (2017), Residents' Barometer 2016 – Survey on Urban Residential Environments, Reports of the Finnish Environment Institute, 19/2017.

Strode, Hudson (14 January 1940), '*Sisu*: A word that explains Finland', *New York Times*, New York, NY: New York Times Company.

Strömsholm, Sonja, Lahti, Emilia, Järvilehto, Lauri, Koutaniemi, Meeri (2015), *Sisu: tarinoita itsensä ylittämisestä ja hyvän tekemisestä*, Jyväskylä, Finland: PS kustannus.

Stubb, Alexander (2013), *The Power of Sisu*, Helsinki, Finland.

Swanson, Anders (12 Feb 2016), 'Icy cycles: the northerly world cities leading the winter bicycle revolution', *Guardian*, London, England: Guardian Media Group.

'The Nordic Countries: The next supermodel' (2 Feb 2013), *The Economist*, London, England: The Economist Group.

The GBD 2015 Obesity Collaborators (6 July 2017), 'Health Effects of Overweight and Obesity in 195 Countries over 25 Years', *The New England Journal of Medicine*, Massachusetts: Massachusetts Medical Society.

Tipton, Charles M. (2014), 'The history of "Exercise Is Medicine" in ancient civilizations', Advances in Physicology Education,

Katja Pantzar

The American Physiology Association, Volume 38, Issue 2,
Bethesda, MD.

Tourula, Marjo (2011), 'The Childcare Practice of Children's Daytime
Sleeping Outdoors in the Context of Northern Finnish Winter',
Doctoral Dissertation, Oulu, Finland: University of Oulu.

UNICEF Research (2017), 'Building the Future: Children and
the Sustainable Development Goals in Rich Countries',
Innocenti Report Card 14, Innocenti, Florence: UNICEF
Office of Research.

Vattulainen, Tuuli (8 May 2014), '5 vinkkiä, miten välttää
niskakivut', *Helsingin Sanomat,* Helsinki, Finland:
Sanoma Media Finland.

Vuori, Ilkka (2015), *Liikuntaa lääkkeeksi: Liikunta-ohjelmia
sairauksien ehkäisyyn ja hoitoon,* Helsinki, Finland:
Bonnier Group.

Wallman, James (2015), *Stuffocation: Living More with Less,*
London, UK: Penguin Random House UK.

Where to Invade Next (2015), directed by Michael Moore,
Dog Eat Dog Films.

Wicker, Alden (September 2016), 'Fast Fashion is Creating an
Environmental Crisis', *Newsweek,* New York, NY: IBT Media.

Williams, Florence (7 Feb 2017), 'How Just 15 Minutes in
Nature Can Make You Happier', *Time,* New York, NY:
Time Warner.

The following websites also provided invaluable background information:

American Heart Association: **www.heart.org/HEARTORG/**

Cleaning Day: **siivouspaiva.com/en**

Current Care Guidelines, The Finnish Medical Society
Duodecim: **www.kaypahoito.fi**

FILI, the Finnish Literature Exchange: **www.finlit.fi**

Helsingin Sanomat: **www.hs.fi**

Helsinki Sauna Day: **helsinkisaunaday.fi**

International Winter Swimming Association: **iwsa.world**

Kela, The Social Insurance Institution of Finland: **www.kela.fi**

Luke, the Natural Resources Institute Finland: **www.luke.fi/en**

Ministry of Education and Culture: **minedu.fi/en**

National Institute for Health and Welfare: **www.thl.fi/en**

Sisu researcher Emilia Lahti's website: **www.emilialahti.com**

Statistics Finland: **www.stat.fi**

Suomen Latu – The Outdoor Association of Finland: **www.suomenlatu.fi/en**

The Federation of Finnish Allotment Gardens: **www.siirtolapuutarhaliitto.fi**

Finland's National Parks: **www.nationalparks.fi**

The Finnish Sauna Society: **www.sauna.fi**

The Lancet: **www.lancet.com**

The OECD Better Life Index: **www.oecdbetterlifeindex.org**

The UKK Institute: **www.ukkinstituutti.fi/en**

This is FINLAND: **www.finland.fi**

Winter Cycling Federation: **www.wintercycling.org**

World Health Organisation (WHO): **www.who.int**

Yleisradio Oy, the Finnish Broadcasting Company: **yle.fi**

Quoted material was reprinted with kind permission of the authors:

Active Healthy Kids Canada 2014 Report Card on Physical Activity for Children and Youth, *Is Canada in the Running?: How Canada Stacks Up Against 14 Other Countries on Physical Activity for Children and Youth,* Toronto, Canada: Active Healthy Kids.

Heikura Pasi, Huttunen Pirkko & Kinnunen, Taina (2000), *Hyinen Hurmio: Avantouimarin käsikirja,* Helsinki, Finland: Edita Publishing. (*Hyinen Hurmio* is referred to as *Glacial Ecstacy* and the quoted information on the benefits of winter swimming is translated and adapted from the original Finnish-language title with permission of all three authors.)

Järnefelt, Heli (2016), 'Työikäisten hyvän unen avaimet', Terveysliikuntauutiset 2016, Tampere, Finland: UKK Institute.

Mogensen, Klaus Æ. (02/2013), 'The Bicycle – The Future Means of Transporation', *Scenario Magazine*, Copenhagen, Denmark: Copenhagen Institute for Future Studies.

Porter, Michael E., Stern, Scott and Green, Michael, 'Social Progress Index 2016: Executive Summary' (2016), Social Progress Index.

Ruusunen, Anu (2013), 'Diet and depression: An epidemiological study,' University of Eastern Finland, Faculty of Health Sciences, Publications of the University of Eastern Finland, Dissertations in Health Sciences 185.

Sahlberg, Pasi (2015), *Finnish Lessons 2.0: What Can the World Learn from Educational Change in Finland?*, 2nd edition, New York, NY: Teachers College Press.

Shevchuk, Nikolai A. (2008), 'Adapted cold shower as a potential treatment for depression', *Medical Hypotheses*, Amsterdam, The Netherlands.

Strandell, Anna (2017), Residents' Barometer 2016 – Survey on Urban Residential Environments, Reports of the Finnish Environment Institute 19/2017.

Disclaimer: This is my personal story. I am not a medical expert, a personal trainer or a nutritionist. But I am a human being who has struggled with finding a sense of balance and wellbeing. The journey in these pages charts how I have found simple and sensible ways to improve my health by tapping into elements of the Nordic lifestyle in my daily life.